APPREHENDED

Britt Hancock

ENDORSEMENTS

Britt Hancock is a friend and great leader. He knows the importance of an intimate pursuit of God. His journey is one of great courage and determination. In *Apprehended,* you will be encouraged to never stop believing, hoping, and pushing forward for an attainable relationship with God.

John Bevere
Author / Minister
Messenger International
Colorado Springs, Colorado

Over the years we've been asked to endorse many books, but this one aligns with our personal passion for Jesus perhaps more than any other. As ones who interact with many leaders in the Body of Christ ourselves, we realize that some are asking the right questions about how to advance the Kingdom, but few are providing real answers that will provoke us to action like Britt does.

We've known Britt and Audrey for most of our lives, so it was no surprise to us to not only read their life stories that have resulted from a genuine affection for Jesus, but to also be challenged by the depths of wisdom, revelation, and obedience they've learned. We will warn you that their unwavering commitment to follow at all cost is contagious!

Apprehended is a book that will touch you profoundly and at times may even make you angry, only to leave you with one way forward—a life spent on Jesus. We can confidently say this will become another classic must-read for Christians, no less valuable than the historical works by other great missionaries of past generations.

It's time for a tsunami of radical lovers of Jesus to be released en masse into the harvest that awaits, ones who refuse to be motivated by anything other than the heart of the Father that all may know Him.

Johnny and Elizabeth Enlow
Speakers and authors of *The Seven Mountain Prophecy,*
The Seven Mountain Mantle, Rainbow God: The Seven
Colors of Love, and *The Seven Mountain Renaissance*
Los Angeles, California

We defeat the enemy by the blood of the Lamb and the word of our testimony. This book and Britt's heart and walk with Jesus are an amazing journey that will inspire you to see and feel our Savior Jesus, beloved Yeshua! Shalom.

Jamie Doss
CEO / Founder, Bethesda Skin Care
Townsend, Tennessee

From the first moment I met Britt Hancock thirty years ago, he has been in "GO" mode! He is driven by the calling to see people transformed by the living Gospel of Jesus. It is an honor for me to recommend this book and, more importantly, the man. This is the story of his living and amazing testimony of a "can't be denied" longing, passion, and drive to see people come to know and be transformed by a relationship with Jesus.

This book is not a glossy inspirational look at the Great Commission. This is a challenge and calling from the very core of Jesus' heart to each of us to reach out and share the power of His truth.

Chris Thomason
President / CEO, in:ciite media
Franklin, Tennessee
inciiteevents.com

Britt Hancock has been my close personal friend for nearly twenty-five years. No other person on the planet encourages me to pursue the Lord and His Kingdom more than Britt. This book is not overdramatized for effect, to make a point, or keep one's attention. It is the life and times of the Hancock family. Every page will challenge the reader to want to know Our Heavenly Father more.

Mark Marble
Senior Pastor
Castle Rock Bible Church
Castle Rock, Colorado

I have had the pleasure of calling Britt Hancock an inspiration and friend for seventeen years. He is in love with Jesus. I don't know anyone who is sold out to a greater degree to relationship with Jesus Christ and His parting admonition to His Church in Matthew 28:19. These pages give you a glimpse of what that passion, under the hand of the Holy Spirit, can accomplish.

Pat Schatzline, Sr.
Daystar International Ministries
Northport, Alabama

As I began to read this book the Holy Spirit began rushing me faster and faster to read what was next. I felt myself being drawn closer and closer to Jesus. This book will become a great teaching tool for me as I minister to people on mission trips.

Henry King
President, King Consultants
Lubbock, Texas

This is an account of the story of Jesus written through the life of my friend, Britt Hancock. It is a story of passion to live out the Purpose of Jesus and to find His Plan to fulfill it. As you read, you will be challenged to be an intimate partner with the King of the Universe, empowered to be a history-maker for the future.

Rusty Nelson
Lead Pastor
The Rock Family Worship Center
Huntsville, Alabama

As Jesus' followers, we're hardwired to want to learn from people who live extraordinarily. Britt Hancock is such a man, embodying Scripture's truth that "you shall find me when you seek me with all your heart." In *Apprehended* there is more truth, insight, and practical motivation than I've come across in years. Follow this man as he follows Christ!

Rob Brendle
Lead Pastor
Denver United Church
Denver, Colorado
www.denverunited.com

There is something powerful about seeing God's supernatural power at work in the raw. Join my friend, Britt Hancock, as he takes you on a real life journey of faith, obedience, and great adversity. See the power of God at work through a man who has truly been APPREHENDED!

Joel Stockstill
Director
BethanyInfluence

This book is filled with life stories of Britt and Audrey's experiences of hope, healing, miracles, and obedience, and you will literally find it to be an instruction manual for ministry. It's as if you are eating a buffet of Truth from the King's table. It will draw you and convict you to walk at a higher level of obedience to the call of God on your life.

The transparency and honesty in this book are so needed in today's modern writings so that the reader cannot only be compelled to know Him more, but to know that it is possible to know Him more. Get ready to GO DEEPER as Britt takes you on an adventure of a lifetime into the fields ready for harvest.

Scott S. Schatzline
Senior Pastor
Daystar Family Church
Northport, Alabama

If you want to read one of the greatest books on how to live and stand by faith, obedience, and miracles; how to face and overcome struggles and intense opposition in life; how to overcome huge obstacles; the joy that comes from total trust in God; how to pray when everything looks hopeless and even dead; and how to see the power of God released, then you want to read this book about the adventures of a modern-day apostolic leader and his family.

Apprehended will take you to new levels of faith and challenge you to believe not only for the impossible but to live a life with purpose that is packed with excitement! If you desire to live a boring Christian life, this book is not for you but if you desire to live a life that makes a difference, this book is your manual to become a world changer!

Al Brice
Senior Pastor
Covenant Love Church
Fayetteville, North Carolina

The Christian life can be summed up in the words hear, believe, and obey. In this book you will be inspired and challenged to live for God in just that way. You will be challenged to assume your role in advancing the work of God in people's lives and you will see firsthand how that has been done in every aspect of Britt Hancock's life and family. This book is a fantastic read!

Tom Lane
Dallas Campus Pastor / Lead Executive Senior Pastor
Gateway Church
Southlake, Texas

Rarely have I read a book that so stirred my faith, pushed my heart to adventure, and reminded me that we must live consumed by Jesus like the book, *Apprehended,* written by my friend Britt Hancock!

This book is destined to be a classic and required reading for everyone who chooses a life of consecration. The cry from within to be used by Jesus is melded into every page!

This book made me want to sell all, grab a backpack, and march into the unknown screaming, "Jesus saves!" If you decide to read this book, I must first warn you to lay down all of your agenda and personal aspirations before you begin the first page! THIS IS YOUR NOW!

Patrick H. Schatzline
Evangelist and Author
Remnant Ministries International

CONTENTS

Foreword

"Who are these people, and what is this bizarre music they are listening to?" I thought to myself as I scanned the smiling faces gathered around the living room of a small condominium in the spring of 1987 at Auburn University.

I was attending the organizational meeting of a Spring Break trip I had signed up for at the student union. I was excited about going skiing again for the first time since I was a kid, but something was different about these people; there was talk of enjoying serving each other on the trip—how ridiculous. And the music—it was haunting and completely unrecognizable. For me, with an almost lexiconical knowledge of secular music, this was unfathomable.

My anxiety was rising along with my pulse and suddenly I realized the horrifying truth: they were Christians! And I couldn't stand Christians. And there was one person, in particular, who made me extremely uncomfortable. His eyes seemed to hold lightning barely contained, and something inside of me, attached to me due to the dark things I was pursuing, was terrified. I wanted to run, to bolt. I anxiously scanned the room for the quickest way out, and at the first opportunity I took it, escaping their company, the Keith Green music that assaulted my senses, and those fiery eyes that seemed to look right through my soul.

Those eyes belonged to Britt Hancock, at that moment number one on my people to avoid list, but soon to become my mentor and discipler, and to this day one of my dearest friends. Thankfully, I was unable to get my money back from the student union, so I reluctantly decided to go on what became a life-changing trip to Colorado in a caravan with a bunch of people who knew Jesus, not just knew about Him.

I found myself standing on his doorstep a couple of months later, "Man, I feel like God wants me to hang out with you," I said. "Good," he responded warmly, "God told me you were coming." His eyes still held an amazing intensity, but what I felt in them then was love, love and an intimate knowledge of the One I had waited a lifetime to meet.

I could see and smell Jesus on Britt, and as we spent time together reading, praying, and talking, his deep commitment to intimate relationship with God, a relationship that you experience, not just believe in, was deeply ingrained in me. I was *apprehended*, and remain so to this day, in no small part due to Britt and his influence on my life.

As you read the pages of this book, the stories of Britt and his family's walk with Jesus, some of it may seem hard to believe. On the surface, many stories in the Bible are the same way. Some of it may seem a bit extreme. Likewise for many passages in the Bible. It turns out that God has not changed, that He is still doing the things He has always done, and that He is knowable, experience-able.

As Britt helped me come into this knowledge and experience of the Most High God, may this book do the same in your life. As you read it with an open heart, may God speak to you, and draw you, and may you be apprehended into fruitful, enduring, intimate relationship with Jesus!

> Collin Cumbee
> Pastor
> Mariners Church
> Irvine, California

Acknowledgements

To Audrey, the love of my life and my wife of twenty-eight years. This book, in the form that it is in, simply would not be possible without your years of patience with me as my writing teacher as I struggled to learn clear articulation through writing. It would not exist like it does without your tireless encouragement these past eight years of its writing, and without the many constant hours you spent editing and re-editing this book. The substance of this book would not exist without your steadfast love for me and the kids and living in daily harmony with me as we ran forward into the unknown, hand in hand. You are truly my RIB.

To my children, Hannah, Aspen, Jacob, and David. You lived all of this with your mother and me. This is OUR story. Without you, my life would be utterly different and void of such rich fulfillment. If no one else reads this book, all the effort it took to write it was worth it just for you to have. I love you forever!

To Mom and Dad, Trey and Kim, and in memory of our sister, Kathy. Thank you. Thank you for being the best family anyone could ever wish for. Thank you, Mom and Dad, for raising us to love God and work hard, and play harder. So many people have regrets concerning their families being dysfunctional. Thanks to the Lord Jesus, and all of you, we have always had an incredible harmony in our family. Thank you for always believing in me and supporting me in all of my adventurous endeavors! We are truly a family blessed by the Lord!

To all of my coworkers in the gospel throughout the years. We walked tough trails together and have seen God do extraordinary things together. Each of you added invaluable equity to my life.

To all of the many faithful supporters who have stood with my family and me and enabled us through your prayers and resources over the past twenty-seven years. You were the instruments God used to enable the growth of the testimonies contained in this book. You have held us up as we poured out our lives as offerings to the Master. Many people whom you will never have the opportunity to meet here on this earth will approach you in the Throne Room of Heaven and thank you for enabling them to hear the Good News. You have an eternal part woven into our testimony. Thank you.

To all of the national believers we have led to Jesus and had the honor to work with over the years. Our lives are indelibly impacted because of God putting you in our lives. We are forever changed because we know you.

To Bruce Nygren. You were the pry-bar that Jesus used to open my hard head to the idea of writing a book! Thank you for your constant encouragement during the years of writing. I am quite certain that I probably would not have continued through this process if it weren't for you. Thank you for the excellent editorial work you did on this project, and thank you for a friendship that has come from this process.

Highest of all thanks belongs to You, Father God. Thank You for Jesus. Thank You for Your unmovable love. Thank You for YOU. Jesus, thank You for saving me and setting me on Your trail and allowing me to know You. Holy Spirit, thank You for dwelling inside of me, filling me with Your presence, opening my mind, clearly showing me truth from lie, and giving substance to my backbone. Thank You, God, for the sweet fellowship we have shared for most of my life. I could never fill enough pages with how I feel about You, what You mean to me, and what You have forged in me. May I die today that I might live in YOU!

Introduction

I was sitting across from Britt Hancock in a Chili's restaurant on the north side of Colorado Springs getting caught up on family, ministry, and life in general, as friends do who haven't seen each other in a long time. The conversation meandered, and then, as it always does, took a personal turn toward what Jesus was doing in our lives.

Suddenly, in the midst of the conversation, Britt's voice grew louder and more intense, which is not surprising to anyone who knows him. He began to describe an experience with Jesus that he had in a mountain village of Mexico during a worship service with the indigenous people of that area. His eyes began to water as he stared directly at me across the booth, speaking in the most descriptive language that I've ever heard from this self-professed Alabama redneck. He was talking about being consumed with a vision of Jesus that overwhelmed him, that shook him, that transformed him.

I was riveted. I felt a little awkward in this public setting as Britt's intensity increased, but probably not as awkward as the people sitting in the booth next to us. I didn't care. Tears rolled down my cheeks occasionally, as we shared together for three hours. My hunger had turned away from the succulent Chicken Crispers in front of me toward the presence of Jesus as he spoke. I wanted more of what Britt was talking about. My heart was awakened to more power, grace, and truth. I wanted more...No, I *needed* more of Jesus in my life.

This has been Britt Hancock's influence on me over the last twenty-four years. Our journeys have crisscrossed through unique and God-ordained seasons in both of our lives. He was the one who introduced me to a friend of his at *Integrity Music,* which led to several worship recordings for the New Life Worship Ministry. We became lifelong friends through some really wonderful seasons, and especially during a few stretches of great struggle and turmoil.

I have found in Britt a rock-solid ally, confidant, co-laborer, and colleague. Very often when he was in town, he would stop by my office, mostly unannounced, and leave a couple hours later, having made the deposit of friendship and encouragement. Britt and Audrey have listened to my wife, Aimee, and me as we were in the midst of deep despair and disappointment. At several of the most difficult intersections of our lives, in God's sovereignty, they've been there with us, praying for us, loving us, and emboldening us to look to Jesus.

I don't know anyone more committed to relationships than Britt and Audrey Hancock. For years, while they were on the mission field, they would run up tremendous phone bills with calls back to their family, friends, and supporters in America. I was one of those people Britt would call out of the blue, and we'd talk for an hour. Britt is an initiator of friendships and will poke, prod, and push if necessary to engage in meaningful dialogue and connection. He is a true friend in the faith, and our conversations over many years have made a tremendous impact in my life and ministry. Many of those conversations include some of the stories that are now written in these pages. You now have the opportunity to experience the stories that Britt and Audrey have to tell.

As you read this book, I want you to imagine Britt and Audrey as two friends who encourage you in your life journey. Let yourself linger over stories of Jesus' work in their lives and the lives of others. Allow yourself to slowly and intentionally absorb the ideas within these incredible experiences. Listen for the voice of God speaking into your own soul as you share in their journey.

Whether it is the captivating story of the presence of Jesus being revealed to Britt in Chapter 5; the agonizing story of Britt praying for a man to be healed of cancer in Chapter 8; the conflicting struggle of their oldest daughter, Hannah, in Chapter 11; the improbable multiplication of chicken and rice in Chapter 13; or the puzzling role of suffering in our lives in Chapter 21; these stories will move you towards God's purpose in your life. And it's not just a book of stories. It is a book of unmistakable spiritual realities that all of us need to be drawn back to again and again. As a pastor, I see it as a book of a thousand messages, rich and deep, with meaningful life-changing truths embedded in every story.

Years after my Chili's experience with Britt, I remember being with him again for a meal. But this time I was sitting alongside him on a wooden bench inside a dark, cinder block house with a dirt floor and a corrugated metal roof, in a small village deep in the mountain regions of central Mexico. There were no windows or doors, just one light bulb hanging from a wire in the middle of the room, and the slapping sound of tortillas being made by women behind the only internal wall in the one-room structure. We would eat soon enough, but first, a slow and deliberate, even halting, conversation went on around me for at least an hour. Any remnants of my college Spanish classes had long since disappeared from my brain, and so I waited, watched, and prayed under my breath, as I witnessed this missionary "house visit."

Suddenly, and seemingly without warning, I was consumed with the warmth of the presence of God in that dreary, poor, run-down, one-room shack. I was overcome with God's goodness to meet with people all over the world, contextualized, and revealed in their language, and in their culture. The presence of Jesus was in the room right there! He started to touch my heart, and speak to me about His grace and love. Tears flowed silently as I sat and received what Jesus wanted to say to me about His purpose and plans for my life. The Gospel was being shared with that family, and it was penetrating my tired heart as well, in a season of my life that was exceptionally challenging.

God had met me there, without instrumentation for worship, without a sermon that I could understand, and without any of the comforts or contexts of my world back at home. But, His presence was the same. Once again, my story had intersected with Britt's story, and my perspective was enlarged. We were served more tortillas and tamales than I could ever eat that day, but I was filled with a hunger for something else, for Someone else—Jesus.

This is the kind of book you now hold in your hands. These are the stories of a family who have been willing to go anywhere, do anything, and be available for any purpose that comes from the heart of Jesus. Inspiring, challenging, and yet completely accessible to the average Christian, this is not a book of unattainable greatness, or miraculous, untouchable faith, but rather, a narrative of struggle, doubt, submission, adventure, unrelenting grace, and incomprehensible peace.

It doesn't matter where you are in your life, or where you find yourself on your spiritual journey, these stories will be used by the Holy Spirit to *apprehend* you. As you read, you will find yourself hungering for more than Chicken Crispers, or handmade tortillas. You will find yourself hungering for more of Jesus Himself.

> Ross Parsley
> Lead Pastor
> One Chapel
> Austin, Texas

Jesus Is Alive

This book relates the testimony of my life and it continues to grow on a daily basis. Not merely words, but living testimony. To become a living epistle is one of the noblest pursuits we can engage in as believers.[1] This is impossible without God expressing Himself inside of us through a personal and vibrant relationship with Him.

As a Christian I have always gravitated more toward *becoming* than *knowing*. *Becoming* the message more than *knowing* information.[2] I believe that the fundamental ingredient of a personal relationship with Jesus is the ongoing process of becoming a living, breathing message to those around us. *Becoming* creates living testimonies.

Testimonies matter because they are the stories of real people working out their journeys with Jesus. Some people may diminish testimonies because they think testimonies are not at the core of the Kingdom, but testimonies are proof of transformation. If there is no transformation we've not met Jesus, and without meeting Jesus we cannot go to Heaven. Testimonies are the tangible proof of salvation.

Without testimonies there is no victory over the enemy. Sermons teach. Testimonies demonstrate the message. Knowledge is sterile and

---

[1] 2 Corinthians 3:2-3

[2] John 5:39-40

powerless until *applied*. The Holy Scripture, written down and given to us in book form, only works on the human heart when it is either read or heard. It then must be understood and appropriated in a living, breathing life.[3] A testimony of the truth means that a person has, in essence, *become* the message, the living proof of the risen Christ.

It's our desire that as you read this book you will be encouraged by the testimony of the twenty-year journey we walked to arrive at the ability to begin our calling. God has called my wife and me to run together on a journey with God. We are in this three-legged race together.

In 1989 the Lord told us to recruit, train, place, and pastor missionaries.

In 1999 the Lord told us to find workers and help them stay in the field.

In 2009 we founded Mountain Gateway in order to do as the Lord had directed.

We are happy to say that Mountain Gateway is currently recruiting, training, placing, and pastoring ministers.

This is our story, or rather, a collection of some of our stories. It's not told chronologically, but the stories fit next to each other and create a picture like a handmade quilt.

I pray that you hear Him calling to you as you read and that you too will be apprehended.

Welcome.

---

[3] Matthew 5:19

The sending of the Son of God to walk the earth clothed in human flesh was, without a doubt, the ultimate, undeniable, and eternal declaration that God seeks to seize our hearts and captivate our lives with Himself and His purposes. What event could bear more importance? What else could possibly compare with this all-consuming expression of the eternal God's decision to apprehend us and claim us wholly to Himself?

Nothing.

God decided to seek mankind out. More to the point, He decided to seek *you* and *me* out.

In the dawning of my youth, the Spirit of God started weaving a fragrance around me that I have never been able to escape. That fragrance has pulled me forward to a known mystery all my life. The fragrance feeds hope. Hope feeds hunger. Hunger fuels engagement with God.

I long to know Him, to dwell in His presence, to understand His ways, to worship Him, and to do what He asks.

I have encountered God, not because I study diligently or because I am consistent in my seeking of the Ageless One. I encounter Him because He draws me. That same love is drawing you. I encounter Him because my encountering is not defined by *what* I believe, but by *Who* I know. My choice to respond to His drawing in turn causes more drawing, and the cycle moves deeper into Him, powered by endless relationship with Someone who is new every morning.

I'm not saying that belief is not critical—it is indispensable. It is the beginning of our relationship with God. When we are born again, belief is the initial point where knowing Him begins. It shapes our perception of who God is. *Belief precedes knowing.*

But belief without relationship is sterile knowledge that is vulnerable to corrupting ideas. Our *relationship* must not be with our *belief*; our relationship must be with Jesus Himself. As we progress in personal intimacy with Jesus, encounter with Him begins to shape our belief, until *knowing Him precedes our belief.* It is a circular process where belief is the genesis of our knowing and our knowing brings clarity to our belief, which in turn causes us to want to know Him more. The more we *know* Him, the more we *believe.*

What we believe defines the parameters of our relationship with God from our side. It is better if *what* we believe develops from *Who* we are growing to know in an intimate way. That *Who* must be Jesus, the Christ. What we *know* and *believe* must never be in conflict with what He has revealed of Himself in the Word of God, or we are deceiving ourselves.

In the beginning our belief shapes God. In the end God shapes our belief.

Ultimately, *what* must come from *Who. Who* must not come from *what.*

I have found that life in its natural course kills hope; it kills belief; it strangles faith. But the intervention and transformation of our life by Jesus is the denormalizing force that *has* changed, *is* changing, and *will* change our realities on a daily basis.

His entire written message to us declares it. All of our conversations and communion with Him proclaim it. He loves us. He died to move us from normal life to supernatural life.

The Kingdom of God is not about words but about power. Power to transform. Power to heal. Power to change. Power to *become* something that we are not—in order to prove that the truth is a living, breathing reality.

Sadly, too often we accept the "inevitable" condition of a "God-encounterless" life. Life happens and we get injured. Some of us fertilize the rootstock of bitterness placed in our heart by unexplainable tragedies. Defeat defeats us and we lose the spark that ignited possibility.

This is the devil's plan. He wins as long as we stop. Stop what? Stop believing, stop hoping, and stop pushing forward.

We must set our face like flint on Jesus and run, regardless of outcomes, emotions, victories, or defeats. We must be living dead men. We must be rocks that float. We must swallow the storms that rage. We must be people who do not demand of God, but rather people who worship Him regardless of any situation in which we find ourselves.

There is no ultimate defeat in the lives of those who know Jesus.

Many things in this life we cannot fight our way through. There is nothing in this life that we cannot worship our way through.

This life is all about Jesus, our relationship with Him, and nothing else.

Jesus is alive!

And that changes everything.

1

Finding His Sheep

In May of 2003 I climbed in my truck and started driving into the remote mountains of Mexico in search of an area where the Gospel had never taken root.

I always look for people who do not know Jesus, because He is the most incredible God anyone could ever know.

My family and I had moved to Mexico in November of 1997 to work with a well-established mission agency among unreached, indigenous people groups. After six years of learning and growing under mature leadership, I was asked to go find a new area and start a work among indigenous people where the Gospel was not established.

I knew the timing was right. But I was scared.

By the end of May we located a town that had promise. On June 7, Audrey and I moved our four children there to begin working to see the Gospel established in the villages nearby.

The streets in our town continue a centuries-old tradition and remain cobblestone. Ninety percent of the streets tilt to reflect the mountainside they are built upon. Some are so steep that when it rains hard you need a four-wheel drive to get up them.

The sound of stone masons cutting stones by hand for the construction of houses, streets, and buildings can be heard on any given day. Hundreds of buildings have handmade clay tile roofs with wide sidewalk overhangs that protect people from the monsoon rains that can create swiftly running rivers in the streets.

Every Sunday people from indigenous tribes fill the streets, coming to buy and sell their products, as the center of our town is transformed into a market that supports all who make this green mountain region our home. Some vendors from outside the area bring in truckloads of goods and produce. Others may walk for hours, carrying on their backs just one basketful of goods to sell. Some ladies, wrinkled with the passage of time and events, carry only one handful of fruit they hope to sell for a few pesos. Still others bring animals to the market to be sold for slaughter. Some bring two hundred pound bags of coffee cherries laden on the backs of their mules to sell to buyers who buy for little, and sell for much.

So, on many monsoon-filled June and July days I rode my Honda XR 600 motorcycle deeper and deeper into the verdant mountains, looking, reflecting, and asking God: *Where do You want me to go? Who do I start with first?*

This area in Mexico, which is on the same latitude as the Hawaiian Islands, is lush and beautiful, harboring dense tropical rainforests. Color is everywhere, with many species of flowering trees, orchids, and other ornamental plants—all growing wild. There are few spots where the rapidly growing foliage doesn't take over, so the men must continually clear the paths and roads with their machetes. Many of the fence lines have living posts that are made from branches cut from living trees. Those branches can be put in the ground, take root, and become towering trees themselves.

Our home is at 3,100 feet above sea level in the upthrust of the Sierra Madre Oriental mountain range that connects to the Huasteco plateau, one of the highest plateaus in North America. If you drive up into the higher mountains from our town, you reach an elevation of 6,000 feet in about twenty minutes. If you leave town in the other direction, in a half hour or so you arrive at a river that's just 600 feet above sea level.

The biodiversity of these uncelebrated steep mountain slopes is incredible. They are covered with an enormous variety of plants and trees that belies the common picture of Mexico as only a country of cactus and dust. Exotic fruit found only in tropical regions display new and amazing colors, shapes, and flavors to newcomers. Coffee is produced by the thousands of tons. Vanilla and cocoa grow native and wild here, this being their place of origin. Deep canyons, at times shrouded in mist, teem with life: birds of every shape and size; fur bearing animals such as coyotes, deer, mountain lions, jaguars, tejons, picarries, tuzas, and others not common in the United States; reptiles, and insects that can't be numbered. It's a fantastic environment.

When we first moved to this beautiful place I was not as concerned with the wonders of such biodiversity as with the growing ache in my heart. I had climbed on my motorcycle now for six weeks, scouting on daily rides often lasting twelve hours in monsoon rains, cold and heat, my kidneys throbbing and sore from riding on miles of rutted mountain roads. As I rounded curve after curve, I found more and more villages, all of them populated with indigenous people, who in all likelihood had never heard or received the Gospel. I had spent six weeks earnestly praying over where to begin our work. Where would we start? With whom? I had learned a strategy of how to minister to indigenous people, but only God can open up the heart.

I desperately wanted to bring glory to my King. I wanted to honor all the wonderful people and churches that for so many years had sacrificed to support our family as we worked to advance the Gospel in Mexico. Now that I had moved out from the mature mission work I had been a part of for the past six years, I felt the weight of full responsibility on me. No longer did I have coworkers and local pastors to work with.

I felt naked, exposed, out on my own. The proverbial rubber had met the road. *Could I do this?* I wondered. I certainly knew that it is God who builds His Church, but would He use me to do it here in these remote mountains and valleys? Could I surrender to His hand and lay down my life to the end that the lost would be saved and discipled?

Sometimes the Holy Spirit would pierce my heart as I stopped to look over mountain ridges and valleys dotted with village after village, and I would fall to my face beside my motorcycle. Other times, I was overcome with compassion, and pled with Jesus for the ability to reach the places I could see, as well as those that were hidden from sight but I sensed were there.

Many nights I stood on various mountain ridges and looked at flickering lights from hidden villages, wondering how I could reach those who lived there, pleading with God to teach me how to win them. It takes so much time, and equipment, and effort. And now we were alone.

Yet not alone.

One morning during family prayer I had my forehead down on the table in front of me and Jesus said, *"Live according to the pattern I have given you: pray, fast, and worship mostly. And when you leave your house you will see Me work."* He helped me focus on something attainable and filled me with great courage and galvanized my will. This I could do. It's how I'd lived my life for years. My doubt and fear melted.

I could keep seeking God.

I could keep praying.

I could keep fasting.

I could keep worshiping.

There is collateral damage all over the world from failed attempts to bring the Gospel to difficult places, and Mexico is certainly no exception. I did not want to just start a few congregations adhering to academic Christianity. I wanted to introduce people to the presence of God and the demonstration of His power—like the Bible reports and like I had observed in my first six years of ministry in Mexico. While I always rejoice to see the lost come to the saving knowledge of Jesus Christ, I did not want to disciple new believers into just another religious system based solely on doctrinal teaching. I didn't give up my life in the United States merely to propagate academic Christianity, but for the empowering hope that Jesus is the same yesterday, today, and forever.

I knew what was possible because I had seen so many miracles in my life. What I did not know was if Jesus would use me in this capacity. I knew He could, but would He?

So I rode my motorcycle for days, past hundreds of villages, never certain where Jesus wanted me to stop. It would be easier to stop a monsoon with a bucket than to stem the rush of people into hell that is evident in these remote mountains. I knew thousands were slipping into eternity all around me in places that are hard to get to. Could I birth something that would begin to stop the spiritual devastation? Could I do this? Whatever the human part is in this God equation, did I have it? Was I surrendered?

All those thoughts never left me as I rode through some of the most beautiful land on earth. It is curious and sometimes irritating to me that many American Christians look at Mexico only as the neighbor to the south, and that it falls outside of the "fashionable and exotic" missions experience. Yet some of the more pagan areas of Mexico can be driven to in less than eight hours from Texas, New Mexico, Arizona, and California.

The people of Mexico are our closest neighbors. Many statistical experts and missiologists have categorized Mexico as "reached." Most of these "experts" either have never lived outside the United States, or if they did, never entered the focused struggle to make disciples in the cultures I've encountered. Will Jesus ask us at the judgment why we did not love our neighbor enough to bring them the Gospel? If we fail to bring them the Gospel, what reason or excuse can we give to Him? That we allowed these experts to convince us that Mexico was "reached," and therefore our resources should go to other more "needy" areas of the world? Do you think He will be as easily convinced as we were?

Many visitors to Mexico only go to tourist areas or to the major cities. These places are completely different from where we live and work. Even most Mexicans who live in urban centers don't know the Mexico that consists of a population that is about 13 percent indigenous with another 12 percent living in rural areas. This comes to 25 percent of the total population of Mexico marginalized and barely reached with the Gospel—thirty million people with only a handful of Gospel workers that focus on them.

Rarely is it realized how populous the indigenous Mexican world is. Our part of Mexico is a separate nation; in fact, nations within a nation—distinct peoples with different languages, customs, and modes of living. There are over sixty distinct languages and even more subdialects. Spanish is the language of trade and literacy, so it is our common denominator for communicating across the many "first-language" barriers that exist.

So many missions organizations throughout recent history have destroyed indigenous identities the world over. They have "gone into all the world and made people Western" instead of making disciples of Jesus. We don't mess with their identities or traditions unless they are demonic or directly opposed to the Gospel.

Rural church planting work is our dominant focus. These areas are vast and remote, and there are literally thousands of unreached villages hidden in the mountains. There are places that are very difficult to get to, making every type of travel available necessary. We hike, ride motorcycles, and drive four-wheel drive vehicles. It takes months or even years just to locate some of the people. Their obscurity is made more acute because of the church's steadfast refusal to target these unreached and demon-entrenched fortresses.

The discipling of our people happens most frequently hiking with them down trails in the mud and rain, sitting on hard benches or stools in dim huts eating a meal, answering questions, or demonstrating power and compassion.

My heart bleeds for the lost of the world. This includes Mexico.

————

Some of the roads we travel every day are little more than trails, thereby shortening the useful life of our equipment with each rotation of the tires. Most driving hours are spent with the transmission in first gear. Proficiency in maintenance, innovation, and remote tire repair is required in order to be where we say we'll be. Keeping our word is the first example these people have that God Himself is not a liar and is trustworthy. If the truck or motorcycle breaks down, we walk. We occasionally swim swollen rivers. Our feet carry us past where the road stops. We go when we say we will go. Someone representing Jesus must show up. This promise we would die for.

I have measured the annual rainfall in our area at two hundred inches, and all this water makes everything more challenging. At times I find mold growing on the boots that I used three days ago. When the mud deepens, the people expect that we will not come. There are flooding rivers, treacherous trails, bandits, and evil neighbors who want to stamp out the Gospel, but we do not call in sick. Jesus said to go. He said to keep our word, even when it costs us. We are determined to do what we say we will do. We are supposed to be living dead men, dead to ourselves, and alive in Christ.

So we go.

One day I left, yet again, to go scout on my motorcycle. I went to fill up at the only gas station in our county. While there I realized I had left my gloves at home, so I went back to get them. As I pulled up I had no idea my extensive scouting was about to end. Standing in the street outside our home was my wife, Audrey, talking with an indigenous man who was selling his wares.

When I saw what Audrey was negotiating for, it caught my attention and immediately triggered memories from my earliest childhood of Big Daddy, my grandfather.

My dad's dad was bigger than life itself. He was physically big, but more than that, he had a big personality that dominated whatever room he was in. He was full of laughter and had a benevolent heart. I'll never forget the times I climbed into his great big car with my cousin, Billy, to go shoot ducks on a lake that Big Daddy had made. We always stopped at the stone corner store in Clay, Alabama, and got orange push-ups to eat on the way.

In his home he had "the rumpus room"—a wonder-filled room that displayed many artifacts from his travels—trophy animal mounts, antlers, antique machines, and a lamp—a lamp made from the hide of an armadillo he had shot in Texas. In my mind that lamp embodied the persona of Big Daddy. It was *Hancock*.

He died when I was just four years old, but the tug that I sometimes still feel in my heart reminds me of how big and awesome he was in my life. I have many specific memories of times spent with him, and all of them are good.

I had been praying since arriving in this new place in Mexico for something to let me know I was "home," in the place where God wanted our family to settle for this next phase of ministry. Like Gideon, I was seeking some sort of sign. Not knowing what exactly, I just needed something that would speak to me personally.

The man speaking with my wife was holding an armadillo hide purse. Audrey knew how unique it was to find something made from armadillo, and because of the significance of Big Daddy's lamp, she bought that purse. We didn't need a purse, but my dear wife knew anything made from an armadillo would mean a whole lot to me—she was acutely aware of how very distinctly *Hancock* it was.

I thought the armadillo purse was a cool thing and then drove off to look for more villages, not hearing what the Holy Spirit was saying. I had to wait just a little longer to see the sign that God had sent me.

The next day Audrey and I went to the open-air market to purchase the food we needed for the week. As we were shopping we stopped and ordered some tacos from one of the many street taco stands. While we sat on the sidewalk waiting on our food, the same man who'd sold Audrey the armadillo purse came by. He didn't recognize us, and

Audrey had to remind him that we had bought something from him the day before.

Then he remembered us and we began to have a conversation with him. I learned that his name was Armando,[4] and I spoke to him in the few Nahuatl words that I knew. Spanish was his second language, which he did not speak very well, so he perked up as I used a few words in his native language and showed interest in him.

"Where do you live?" I asked him.

Armando told me the name of his village and asked if I wanted to come to his house!

"Por cierto!" (Of course!) I said in Spanish, amazed at the invitation. As we talked some more I offered to give him and his wife a ride home later that afternoon.

They showed up after the agreed upon time and we rode together to the village nearest theirs. We parked on the road and hiked in the light rain another twenty minutes to their house. We started to talk, and I ended up spending five hours with them. I shared the Gospel, and by the end of that day, Armando gave his heart to Jesus!

This was my sign. The first man to accept the Gospel was the one who brought me a piece of "home." I didn't have to wonder any longer if this was the right area.

This was the place. We would stay here.

––––––––

Many of the villages that we target and work in are small, consisting of just a handful of houses. The biggest village we work in has about two hundred houses, the smallest about ten. The homes are

---

[4] Names have been changed.

spread throughout the jungle, sometimes making it hard to distinguish where one village stops and another one begins. The people know though.

Many houses are built from materials the people can get from the jungle. Grass roofs that last twenty years or more and handmade clay roof tiles shelter the people from the heavy rain. Split bamboo and hand-sawn boards are held together with handmade fibrous cords to create walls that provide a boundary from the surrounding jungle. Floors are often bare rock or tamped earth. Windows do not appear in most walls, as the cracks between bamboo or boards yield a view to the outside.

Many villages have no electricity.

Plumbing, if there is any, consists of a wooden "stob" in the ground with wire holding a spigot that's connected to a black plastic water pipe which snakes its way across the ground or through the trees—sometimes for several kilometers—from an above ground, galvanized water main. Many people still haul water on their heads from springs that only the locals know of.

Firewood for cooking simple meals of beans and corn is hauled mostly on the backs of the young and old. Meals are cooked over an open fire, often on a raised mud platform, so that the women don't have to stoop to stir pots and flip tortillas.

Their living doorbells—

barking dogs or

clucking chickens or

turkeys sounding their

echoing song through

the forest—give away

the location of hidden

dwellings, helping us

locate the lost

and dying.

So many times while hiking through the jungle I come upon a house that I have never seen before. If there is corn growing, that means that Indians live nearby. If a trail is distinct, it usually leads to people.

Two or three generations often live together, hidden by thick vegetation in homes you can't see until you are very close to them. Their living doorbells—barking dogs or clucking chickens or turkeys sounding their echoing song through the forest—give away the location of hidden dwellings, helping us locate the lost and dying.

———

The mountains themselves reveal many mysteries, dangers, and rewards. Dangers to those who refuse to see and hear; rewards to the patient and sent. Animals of various sizes and kinds take their created place in the mystery. Deer allow fleeting glimpses to only those who know how to see. Peccary root the ground and raise their young living on jungle roots and vegetation. Raccoon, coati, skunk, fox, coyote, and armadillo frequently exist in conflict with people. Occasionally mountain lions, and in some areas jaguars, strike tragedy to children and livestock as they follow their carnivorous instincts. Parrots flock through the overstory of the rainforest and numerous other species of birds add their voices to a rarely silent symphony.

Colonies of leafcutter ants move rapidly about their business, crossing—and sometimes covering—yards of trail, their feet beating tiny roadways that run for miles on the jungle floor. Their movements, which are an open book to those who know how to interpret them, can announce the coming of the rain within twenty-four hours. I have never determined the number of different types of caterpillars that consume leaves and nourish birds and reptiles and mammals. Their widely varying colors dazzle the curious, and their different sizes are surprising on first encounter. Painful, sometimes dangerous, lessons are learned by coming in contact with these beautiful, but poisonous, slow-moving insects.

Plants speak without words by their color and surface sheen, telegraphing which can be touched and which cannot. Some plants nourish and some heal, others will sicken or even kill. It takes time and patience to learn this literacy of nature that does not come from books but is taught by people who would be considered by many to be backward, uneducated, and illiterate.

However, if economies collapse and electronic systems fail, these ordinary and unschooled people will not suffer any drastic change in their lives. They will continue to plant and harvest in an endless rhythm. It is the society of the enlightened moderns that will collapse. These whose hands still have a direct connection to the ground will thrive and may even come to the rescue of those who are more ignorant than they realize.

2

Beginnings

My passion to know God emerged so early in my life that I cannot remember exactly how or when it began.

I spent a lot of time in the great outdoors while growing up in rural Alabama, often wandering for hours by myself through a thousand acres of undeveloped land that surrounded our home in the country-side outside Birmingham. Early on I was influenced by great outdoor experiences—hunting and trapping, skinning and tanning hides. I established my identity in those woods where I always wanted to be—camping, backpacking, shooting my bow, and wandering for endless hours and days.

I grew up in a strong Christian family and was born again when I was six years old. One day when I was eleven, while wandering alone on our family property, I had a forever life-altering encounter with the Holy Spirit. He came upon me, saturated my whole being, and lit a burning fire inside me to know Him and make Him known. That fire still burns in me to this day! I would not trade my upbringing for anything.

I am the youngest of four siblings—nine years younger than my brother, Trey, seven years younger than my sister, Kim, and six years younger than Kathy. My family profoundly influenced me to seek God. I grew up trying particularly hard to follow the example of Trey. He was, and still is, my hero. He read his Bible, so I read mine. He prayed, so I prayed. He had an unquenchable desire to introduce people to Jesus and talked to *everybody* about Him, so I tried to do so as well.

Late at night I would sometimes lie on the floor outside Trey's bedroom door and listen to him cry out in prayer for souls. This had a profound impact on my life. It set a lifelong tone for me—that nothing matters but Jesus...and helping others know Him.

Although I wanted to pattern my life after Trey, I always had an intense drive of my own to know and walk with Jesus. As I grew, everything I learned about the Bible or heard taught in church or experienced in ministry was, and still is, eclipsed by this supreme desire. Jesus is worth more than this life can ever contain. I want my life to be defined by the incomparable presence of God. He is real and will break out of the intellectual boxes where we have confined Him—if we seek Him with all of our heart. I want to walk with God, and nothing else matters to me. And I want to spend the life I have here on this earth helping others to walk with God too.

In 1975 an event occurred in my life that set me up for the testimony and teachings found in this book. I was ten years old, and Trey was about ready to leave for college. He was so big in my world that his looming absence was about to create a huge vacuum in my heart.

The day before he left for Auburn University, he took me in his 1973 Plymouth Duster for a ride that I'll never forget. I had ridden with him many times, but I don't remember any specific ride except that one. I recall vividly the feeling I had, wishing that that ride would never end. My hero was leaving the next day, and I wanted somehow that it not be so.

I remember sitting at a red light in Center Point, Alabama, watching Trey and not saying anything...watching him shift gears, wondering if I would ever have strong hands like his...pulling into the driveway of some of his friends as he went to tell them goodbye...just driving around so that Trey's little brother could have this moment with him.

During that ride Trey told me, "Always look for Jesus. Talk to Him and read the Bible. There's nothing more important."

Trey was always all about Jesus. He still is. So as a boy I did what my hero told me to do. I looked for Jesus. And I found Him.

———

A couple of years after Trey left for college I moved into his bedroom. By that time I had spent a lot of time in those untamed woods that adjoined our house, seeking to find Jesus. I wandered that land daily, not even wanting to leave our property to go to a restaurant to eat. This was my predominant activity until I graduated from high school. My mom tells me that it was like pulling teeth to get me to go anywhere.

It was sometime and somewhere out there on that property that Jesus began letting me find Him. He drew me out there to wander with Him, and wander I did. Once, when I was about eleven years old, I felt His presence so strongly that I was actually afraid that I might see Him. I was scared, so I put my face down in the leaves until the intensity subsided.

I also spent countless hours sitting in Trey's armchair in my bedroom while worship music played. I gazed out the window late at night, praying and waiting for God. I had a Marantz stereo with a LP turntable, cassette tape player, an 8-track player, and four speakers. The Christian music never got turned off, even when I slept. I never listened to secular music. I listened to Keith Green, The Second Chapter of Acts, Barry McGuire, Mustard Seed Faith, Chuck Girard, Joy and Bob Cull, and Maranatha! Music. Even when I went to school in the morning I left the music on. Praise played in my room 24/7.

Night after night, I sat in Trey's chair that faced out the window and I prayed—reaching out to God while the worship music played. Sometimes I sensed the presence of Jesus so strongly, as I had in the woods, that I got down on the floor and hid my face.

I felt Him drawing me towards something, but I wasn't sure what.

Now, years later, I would say that I was being drawn to know and experience the true God, the One who in His *normal* existence is awesomely supernatural. This is His promise fulfilled! If we seek God with all of our heart, we will find Him. If we draw near to Him, He will draw near to us. It is His one greatest hope. It is our deepest fulfillment.

My Miracle

I was still a young man when I had one of my first dramatic personal encounters with the awesome supernatural power of God.

One night, in June of 1984, when I was a freshman at Auburn University, I was up late one night studying for Dr. Lishak's Biology 101 exam when I noticed that I could not see two letters in a long scientific word. I rubbed my eyes but that didn't help. I still could not see the letters. I thought I was just tired so I went to bed.

It turned out I wasn't just tired. From that night it only took two weeks until I lost the central vision core in my left eye, and the vision in my right eye was starting to fade too.

When I could no longer see anything out of my left eye, except peripherally, I figured I better see a doctor, so I walked to the infirmary at the university. I was shown into the exam room and waited while the doctor did whatever doctors do while you sit alone in those antiseptic-smelling rooms.

Finally, the doctor came in and when I told him about the problem with my eyes, he had me sit on the end of the examining table and read the eye chart on the wall. First, he covered my left eye. I could read the top couple of rows, the ones with the biggest letters. He then covered my right eye and all I could see was what seemed a type of black-grey mass blocking my vision. Forget seeing the eye chart. I could almost feel the obstruction, which looked like the dirty cotton out of an aquarium bubbler. I couldn't see anything from that eye, not even the doctor. I was able to catch some movement, but only in my peripheral vision. The central vision core in my left eye was a dark hole in my vision.

When I told the doctor that I couldn't see the chart at all, I sensed his alarm. He asked me how long I had been like that and I told him, "For about a week." That alarmed him even more. He explained to me how his own son had an eye condition where blood vessels had burst inside his eye and suddenly he'd gone blind.

The doctor told me to go home that day and not to drive. He referred me to a specialist, Dr. David Davidson, at the Eye Foundation Hospital at the UAB medical complex in Birmingham. I got some friends to drive me two and a half hours the next day to my family's home, and my parents immediately made an appointment with Dr. Davidson.

A few days later my parents and I arrived at Dr. Davidson's office. I had a knot in my stomach as I signed in on the clipboard. I was nervous. I had a real problem and I needed real power to fix that problem. Waiting to see the doctor must have been the longest thirty minutes of my life up to that time.

Just before I'd gone blind, I'd had a particularly intense time of prayer with the Lord. For the first time in nine years of prayer He had begun to give me some clarity about what He wanted me to do with my life. I knew that I had to serve Him with all that was in me. He had put

His mark upon my heart from the time I was eleven years old. Now He was finally letting me see the beginning of His pathway for me—the path I am still on. He had told me clearly that I was going to be tested, but not to give up...that an attack was coming and that I should draw up battle lines.

Problems are opportunities for faith. You don't really know if you have faith until there is a reason for faith.

> Problems are opportunities for faith. You don't really know if you have faith until there is a reason for faith.

When I had arrived home from Auburn, getting ready for the appointment with this eye specialist, we had called everybody we knew and asked them to pray. Because of the positions my siblings held with several ministries, there were thousands of people all across the United States praying.

The doctor came to greet us in the waiting room, and even as he introduced himself, I sensed something unique about him—I felt Jesus in Him. We followed him to his office and after we sat down, he explained what we were about to do. We then went to an exam room where he immediately went to work. He introduced me to his head nurse, and she had me lie down on the exam table where she put those stinging dilation drops into both of my eyes. The doctor then began to question me about what the problem was, gleaning his questions from the medical questionnaire we had filled out upon arriving. He also had the doctor's report from Auburn.

After he got through the medical history, my eyes were fully dilated and his nurse came in with an IV. She inserted the needle and ran a yellow dye into my blood vessels. We then walked out of the exam room, down the hall to the elevator and up two floors to have pictures taken of the inside of my eye. This process was not a blessing! There was a mechanical device to help me hold my eyelid open while the camera strobe flashed more than a hundred photographs of the inside of both of my eyes.

It felt odd having to be led back down the stairs since I could not see out of one eye and the other one was dilated blurry. I wondered through a growing knot in my stomach if this was to be my future, having to be led around by others for the rest of my life. The thing that brought me the most sadness was the thought of never being able to see the mountains again.

We sat in the doctor's office and talked about symptoms and conditions that are likely in situations like these, details and options and what if's—information intended to educate and bring clarity to those who are subject to bad news, information that impacts lives and changes dreams and plans and life function. Some of this conversation with my doctor I do not remember because I was distracted by the wonderings in my own heart about what was happening to me.

I vividly remember when the doctor stepped out to read the photographs of the inside of my eyes. Great sadness and concern became tears and made their way down my mother's face. That was my first glimpse at the pain parents feel when their child has a serious health problem.

The doctor returned and began to relate what he thought my issue was. He believed I had macular dystrophy, a genetic disease that affects the central vision core of your eye. In essence, something in my genes had triggered the cells in my macula to die. The left eye was the most dramatically affected, and there was nothing that they could do for my advanced condition. The doctor told me that he was almost certain that the condition was in my right eye also, which concerned him the most. He wanted to consult with some other specialists before he gave a final diagnosis.

There were some things that he felt did not make sense about my situation. One was my age of nineteen; it was rare for someone so young to get this disease. Another was that since this was a genetic problem, why did we know of no one else in the family who had it? So Dr. Davidson wanted to get some other doctors to study the data. He sent us home to await his phone call.

Waiting for such calls is agonizing. We called more people to get them to pray. We called those already praying with an update. We prayed and prayed, and I did not sleep very well.

Two days later, at 11:00 p.m., the phone rang. It was Dr. Davidson and he confirmed his suspicions, the diagnosis was macular dystrophy. He explained that there was ongoing research in genetic engineering that could possibly bring a cure at some time in the future. He wanted me to make a trip to the Bethesda Institute in Maryland where they were conducting leading edge research on my disease.

"I am sorry, Britt," he said. "There is nothing that I nor anybody can do for you medically."

I told him that we believed that God could heal and that there were thousands of people praying for me. He told me he was glad to hear that because he, too, was a born-again Christian and believed in miracles and that God could heal me. "I'll pray for you too, Britt." Then we hung up.

My parents were heartbroken. It is a terrible thing when one of your children is stricken with something that cripples or kills. They did not want me to return to Auburn, but I could not just sit at home and give up, surrendering to despair while my sight faded away, so my parents graciously allowed me to return to school.

Jesus had given me my first marching orders for ministry, and I had launched a prayer initiative for the campus having to do with world prayer and evangelism. I had to go back. I knew I was in a spiritual fight—Jesus had warned me a test was coming! I did not really know how to fight, but I knew it would be a mistake to just acquiesce to the sadness.

While growing up, I had been taught of the healing power of God from the Bible and had heard so many testimonies about healing. My sister, Kim, had been healed of scoliosis while she was at Auburn seven years earlier. Others had been healed at our church. I had heard countless stories from visiting missionaries of how God was still working wonders in their ministry. Now I had the opportunity to see Him work a miracle in my own life.

Every miracle that I have ever seen has come because of a problem.

Every miracle that I have ever seen has come because of a problem.

I returned to school, vainly trying to stay in my classes. All my professors were kind and offered to let me out of the bad grades I was making as a result of going blind. They all told me that if I just would not take the final exams that none of the classes would count. Maybe I should have listened to them because I failed half of my classes that quarter, killing my GPA. But from a spiritual standpoint, I knew I couldn't quit.

During the time that I couldn't see I spent more time with Jesus than at any other time in my life. Such a spiritual hunger spooled up inside of me. I certainly wanted my sight back, but more than anything else I wanted to know Jesus—more than succeeding in school, more than a career, more than life. I wanted to walk in His power the way I'd read about in the Bible, the way my home church had taught me was possible. I told Jesus that if He did not heal me, I was going to quit school and start preaching full time. I'd known that I was called to preach from the time I was fourteen years old.

But the more I sought Jesus, the worse my eyes got. I determined to demonstrate joy in every situation, and to be patient in my affliction. I was not going to be preoccupied with my disease, so all my seeking centered on knowing the Healer and not the healing. I did ask Him to heal me, but I refused to be dominated by sickness.

I poured myself into other people as much as I could, witnessing, praying, talking, and rallying people in the prayer and evangelism initiatives on campus. Some well-meaning believers caught wind of what was happening to me and told me to "confess my healing" and not say anything negative about the situation with my eyes. I didn't buy this. To me, if you say you can see when you can't, that's not a positive confession—it's a lie. If the problem weren't real, then neither would the miracle that fixed it be real.

One Sunday morning I slept through church because my friends and I had been out playing hide-and-seek in the campus arboretum till late the night before. They had chosen to play at night so that I would not be the only one with a disadvantage. I awakened late that morning and noticed that my eyes seemed even worse.

It was exam week and I went to the house of some friends to try and study. I got up from the table where we were studying and walked outside the front door to stretch. I turned to go back inside, and as I crossed the threshold, my sight came back in an instant! Outside I'd not been able to see, inside I could!

Stunned and bewildered, I turned and went back outside. I looked to the left, three blocks up W. Glenn Avenue, and *I could SEE* the stop sign on the corner of N. College Street! AMAZING!

I went back inside the house and calmly began to tell my friends that I could see. Well, maybe it was calmly at first, but before long the shouting started. I was ecstatic!

It took three months before I quit blinking and rubbing my eyes. Being able to see clearly out of *both* eyes was, and still is, a marvel.

I've now seen mountain ranges on three continents. I can see my wife, my children, and my grandchildren. My heart is full of gratitude. Jesus healed me! He is ALIVE!

3

Deeper

There is a difference between *plans* and *purpose*. Purpose is an end to be obtained, an outcome if you will. A plan is a *means* to accomplish a purpose, a tool utilized to arrive at an outcome. When it comes to God and His utilization of plans to accomplish His purpose in our lives, so many get lost because of the difference in meaning between those two words.

We can see this illustrated quite clearly when God spoke to Abraham and told him to sacrifice His son Isaac.[5] God gave Abraham a plan (sacrifice your son) in order to reveal what was really in his heart (Did he truly fear God?). It is clear to us that God did not intend for Abraham to kill his son, but He issued the order without explanation. God used this plan to affect His purpose.

God still utilizes this basic pattern with each of us. He may send us to do something in order to reveal something entirely different. It was something akin to this that God did in my life to lead me through multiple steps to the mission field.

When I was healed of macular dystrophy my resolve to keep following Jesus strengthened. Up to that point I had been seeking my destiny

---

[5] Genesis 22:1-12

with God to the best of my ability. That destiny had been born early in my life through time spent in prayer, worship, and countless hours wandering alone in the woods surrounding our home.

Then, while at Auburn University, the Holy Spirit slowly began to craft definition to His destiny for me during times of deep solitude, as I sought God with all of my heart and wrestled to allow Him control of every facet of my life. My single-purpose heart gained sharp focus during my time at Auburn. I resolved to be "all in." No matter what I would do, it must be done with all of my heart "as unto the Lord."[6]

The accomplishment of God's purpose for each of us includes many plans and stepping-stones.[7] If we set ourselves to follow Him, we will be led by Him to many locations for many reasons, and all those reasons will work together to fulfill His purpose in us. We have a destiny in God, and fulfilling that destiny involves preparation and multiple steps.[8]

When I was a senior in high school, I was faced with the decision of all high school seniors—"what now?" My pastor thought I should go to Bible school. It seemed obvious to him that I had a call to preach (which I did), so the expected plan for me, in his mind, was for me to go to Bible school and then, possibly to seminary. Isn't that what you do if you are called to preach? This is a very common assumption. This is so often the default thinking. But God doesn't function by default. Everything He does is purposeful and tailored for each person.

This is the primary difference between *religion* and *relationship*. He has purpose and destiny for each of us and an endless supply of plans; each designed to bring about our cooperation and the terminus of His purpose.

---

[6] Colossians 3:17, 23

[7] 2 Corinthians 3:18, Romans 1:17

[8] Psalm 37:23

Relationship means that we don't automatically assume default thinking is the will of God. He must be consulted first. Sometimes His answer coincides with established expectations. Sometimes it does not. The point is, we should never just assume anything. We should bring everything to God in prayer. If He does not answer (and sometimes He does not because He wants to watch how we make decisions), then we must weigh our decisions with the nature of God.

I truly wanted to follow God and knew that He had a calling on my life, but I just did not know what to do after high school. My parents and I went to Tulsa, Oklahoma, and toured Oral Roberts University. I also knew about Evangel College and Southeastern Bible College, because we had attended an Assemblies of God church while I was growing up. All of these are fine schools, but I was not attracted to any of them.

I was conflicted and could not make a decision. As long as I tried to hear from the Lord and assimilate information to make a wise decision, I was in turmoil. Thank the Lord Jesus for that turmoil! It kept *me* from making a plan and ensured that I stayed the course to find out from God what plan *He* had for my next step. What an unmitigated disaster it would have been if *I* had decided to make a plan about what to do and where to go.

I realize now that this was my first real point of surrender. At the time I still mistakenly believed that "counting the cost," meant "knowing the details." I thought that once all the details were collected I would know my options and could simply pray and seek wise counsel in order to make an informed and wise decision.

Sometimes God steps back and watches our decision-making process and does not speak until after we have made a decision because He wants to see if we will follow His ways. It is not wrong to gather information and pray and seek counsel, and many times I sort through things this way, but the details and counsel should never *replace* the voice of God.

After finishing high school I didn't want to bring to God my options and try to get Him to bless *my* plan for my life. I wanted to know *His* plan for my life and follow that. The bottom line is that God very often doesn't give many details. He knows what He wants, but faith demands that we walk forward without knowing everything. I stumbled through this process and somehow heard God.

I talked with my brother, Trey, and he encouraged me to really seek the Lord and find out a yes or no answer from Him. He actually warned me that if God did not want me to attend Bible college, then going there would be a mistake. Trey told me how he had walked that path by going to a Bible college and it had taken him ten years to get some of the nonsense he had learned there out of his head. So I decided to really seek God and find out what He wanted. If Jesus wanted Bible college for me, then off I would go! If He had another plan, that is what I wanted to know.

Human reasoning is thin ice upon which to build your life. In trying to make a wise decision, we can collect exhaustive details and counsel about a situation and still make the utmost mistake…and miss hearing and doing what the King of kings says to do. The details can drown out His voice.

So, as a senior in high school, I set myself up to seek Jesus and hear Him. And as soon as I decided to lay down all of the information and details and reasons and lock into His presence and seek His voice, He spoke to me. He said quite simply, "Go to Auburn University." I was thrilled! That was what I had wanted to do all along.

Next I asked God what I was supposed to study. He said, "It doesn't matter what you study. Study whatever you want to study. It is not about what you study. It is while you are there in school that I will reveal the beginning of the road of your calling."

Such peace flooded my soul. I went to Auburn. *War Eagle!*

Although I was accepted for the fall quarter of 1983, I did not begin school immediately. Instead, my dad and I took a long promised trip to Wyoming to hunt pronghorn antelope. I entered Auburn in January of 1984 for the winter quarter.

At the beginning of that spring quarter Jesus began to really stir me spiritually. I was drawn into times of deep prayer, and He began to speak to me strongly about things I had never considered. One thing was a strong burden to pray for the students and faculty. I began to visit various campus ministries and make friends with believers from many faith backgrounds. The segregation and lack of unity among groups was very loud in my spirit, and I saw the lack of spiritual depth in students. They had little real zeal for winning the lost, yet many of them had a strong Bible base, having grown up in church. As Jesus stirred me, I began to do my best to stir others. Out of that stirring, clarity emerged.

I was appalled by the prayerless state of believers. Right before I went blind Jesus gave me the names of sixteen people He wanted to call together on a regular basis. He told me not to say anything to them and that He would bring them to me. He prompted me to launch an initiative to draw together those sixteen students from different backgrounds to hunger for God's presence and really pray for souls. Within two to three weeks every one of those people came to me on their own and asked about getting together. We called ourselves, "The Servants."

The next quarter, summer of 1984, is when I went blind and was healed. I was nineteen years old and had walked with God for thirteen years. That trial was the first real test of my resolve to be unshakable in trusting in Jesus—the first difficult faith challenge in my life. It would prove to be the first of many similar opportunities to develop faith.[9]

---

[9] James 1:2-4

One thing led to another as we began to pray. Suicide was a problem at Auburn at that time, especially during final exams. One night during finals our group of friends was playing hide-and-seek in Haley Center, a building with nine stories, the tallest on campus. Haley Center is the head-quarters of the Liberal Arts College, and on its top floor there used to be meeting rooms surrounded by an open balcony called the "Eagle's Nest."

We used to go up there to study, throw water balloons at people (don't tell), and sometimes have Bible studies and other functions. The building complex consists of the central tower and four quadrants off the four corners of the central tower. Those quadrants are four stories tall with big courtyards between them. The courtyards are open to the sky, easily viewed from the Eagle's Nest above.

While our group was playing that night someone jumped off the Eagle's Nest and hit the ground nine stories below in one of the court-yards. Apparently, he was in such despair over his final exams that he jumped to his death.

Our group found him. It was so sobering, and we were overcome with righteous indignation at the enemy for deceiving yet another person to take his life. We decided to get even more serious in our inter-cession for the campus and really blanket the school and the town with prayer against despair, deception, and the spirit of suicide.

We went all over the campus and prayed and anointed many places with oil, including the Eagle's Nest. There had been a string of suicides on campus spreading over several years, and we cried out to God to stop people from taking their own lives.

The suicides stopped and there were no more for years and years.

Dare to pray. Do it with faith. It works.

Across the street from the apartment where I lived was an abandoned building, and a witchcraft coven was meeting on the second floor. Several of us had been in there and seen a big pentagram drawn out on the floor, candles at each point of the pentagram, and all manner of vile and satanic writing on the floor and walls.

After we discovered this and started praying, we went in the building, smashed the candles, and poured a gallon of oil all over the pentagram. Then we prayed that God would save the participants and put a stop to their meetings.

The meetings did stop, and a Christian purchased the building and built apartments on the second floor. The owner donated retail space on the first floor for a Christian bookstore and Sav-A-Life, a Christian pregnancy resource center.

Prayer works.

Hunger for God increased on campus and we began to see God stirring people from all backgrounds. God started sending freshmen to Auburn who burned with a passion for God. Lukewarm "churchians" caught on fire for God and groups began to form that focused on unity. At one point we could call an all-night prayer meeting and have two hundred students show up. From that group at Auburn many went out all over the United States and world to follow God. We are some of those students.

Marriage and Ministry

In November of 1986, a longtime friend, Sissy Costner (now Boone), came over to my apartment for dinner. She told me about a friend of hers named Audrey and said I just had to meet her. We were headed to a Bible study after dinner, and Sissy asked if we could go by the dorm to pick up Audrey. So we did, and down the steps walked the woman who is now my rib!

She was wearing a forty-year-old grey sweatshirt of her Granddaddy's, cutoff blue jeans, and bunny slippers (she still has those bunny slippers). She got in the backseat of my Toyota Camry, slid over my buckskin pants and the deer antlers, and said to me, "You remind me of my brother."

Sissy jumped on the inside! Audrey had just told Sissy that she wanted to marry someone like her brother, someone who loved the outdoors and could work with his hands.

Audrey and Sissy became a part of a prayer group I was leading that met at my apartment five mornings a week before class. Audrey and I got to know each other's hearts and spirits as we began our friendship. Jesus forged our hearts together in that prayer group, and the storms and victories of the last twenty-eight years have only served to deepen and temper the bond Jesus began to build in us in 1986.

In July of 1987 I attended a church service in Auburn that dramatically impacted the direction of my life. Preaching that night was a missionary from Mexico named David Hogan. I was astonished at how simple his message was, and how he shared about the power of God. I had to find out more about him and felt that Jesus was assigning me to pray for him. So in January of 1988 I took a trip through Mexico into Guatemala with him.

That trip began to turn my heart from a focus on the United States outward to the world. It added more fuel to my spiritual fire, and Jesus began to work missions into my heart. I began to pray more fervently every day for David Hogan and all of the missionaries in his ministry, Freedom Ministries. The more I prayed, the more my heart turned to the world and its lost state.

Audrey and I got married in March of 1988 during her spring break, less than a month after my return from that mission trip and sixteen months after we met. We got back from our honeymoon and jumped into ministry with all of our strength. Audrey had five quarters left at Auburn and she got her degree in Elementary Education while I worked as a builder in my dad's construction company.

We made the leap into full-time ministry and started to live on support in August of 1989, when Audrey was five months pregnant with our first child, Hannah. We took a trip to Yellowstone National Park for a few weeks to have a dedicated time of prayer and fasting. It was there that God first spoke clearly to me to train missionaries. I was given that assignment on top of an unnamed mountain southwest of Hedges Peak. It both scared and excited me. We returned to Auburn with fresh fire and a more specific direction for our life and ministry.

Our apartment became a ministry center. People were always there praying, receiving prayer, asking questions, dreaming, and being challenged to seek God with all they were worth. Audrey and I challenged each other, and there has never been another ambition or focus for us other than following Jesus.

We decided to set an empty place at our table for meals in case Jesus wanted to send people over for us to minister to. I remember very few times that place being empty. So often for breakfast, lunch, and dinner we were feeding someone hungry for Jesus. They were hungry for Audrey's cooking as well.

Audrey, ever the evangelist and a person of great caring, started a ministry to the cleaning staff of Haley Center. It began when the Lord told her to bake cookies for one of the maids she had made friends with. She wanted to say thank you to her and others for cleaning the floors and classrooms.

It grew to be a weekly ministry. Audrey baked banana bread and made a pitcher of Gatorade, which we took to the staff once a week. The maids and janitors were somewhat suspicious at first, but as we developed a relationship with them, they started letting us pray with them. After about a year and a half of consistency, we were able to start a short Bible study one day per week with all of the cleaning and maintenance crew at their lunch break. That led to invitations to some of their homes in the government housing project where most of them lived.

We were working with students every day, living on support, figuring out that trusting God for everything works, even when you are pregnant and have no health insurance, then have a new baby. Jesus proved His faithfulness in all things, and He has never stopped.

Audrey and I launched an initiative for praying for the world. We had students meeting five days a week at 6 a.m. and we used the World Prayer Map from Every Home for Christ to systematically pray for every country of the world. For years we prayed five days per week for God to send out workers into the harvest. The seed of nations was planted in our own hearts, because of all those hours spent calling out to God for the world. We did not know what we were doing, but God knew what He was doing.

We also completed our first faith project: a World Prayer Center with three rooms for groups to systematically pray for world evangelism and five rooms for individual prayer that was available 24 hours.

I made multiple trips with David Hogan to Latin America, including Mexico, Guatemala, Bolivia, Peru, and Paraguay. Every trip served to place more things in my heart from God. I was weighed down with a burden to pray for the missionaries of Freedom Ministries, and especially for David Hogan.[10] God was speaking to me often and sometimes

---

[10] 2 Corinthians 11:28

keeping me up at night or waking me up in the early morning to pray, especially about missionaries who had left or were leaving the field. I was seeing a deeper glimpse of His heart for the lost state of the world.

During one of those early morning, deep prayer times with Jesus, I had a vision concerning raising prayer support focused on the missionaries of Freedom Ministries. I saw a plan unfold having to do with traveling with David Hogan when he visited churches across the United States. The Hogans agreed to this plan, so in February of 1992, only six weeks after our second daughter, Aspen, was born, we joined the Hogans and traveled on a six-month tour of the United States, doing our best to recruit a prayer team to pray for Freedom Ministries on a systematic basis.

On the first Sunday night of March, David preached at New Life Church in Colorado Springs, Colorado, where we met Ross Parsley who was the church's new worship pastor. The Holy Spirit touched Audrey and me personally, and we really felt a connection to the church. Within the next few days, God spoke to both Audrey and me and told us basically the same thing: "You are to move to Colorado Springs. New Life is to be your church, and Ted Haggard will be your pastor, elder, and friend." We had more months of traveling with the Hogans, but we began to pray about this new direction.

In May we had a break in our trip, so we went to Colorado Springs to investigate places to live, as well as to meet with Ted Haggard to see if he would support us moving our ministry to Colorado Springs. We had a good meeting with Ted and located an apartment.

We resumed our travel schedule with the Hogans and continued raising a prayer team to pray for Freedom Ministries, while trying to get things in order at Auburn to unhook our lives there and move fourteen hundred miles to Colorado. As it turned out, God worked things out with the Prayer Center and it ran for years after we left, totally led by students.

We moved to Colorado Springs in September of 1992 and jumped into life and ministry at New Life Church. What God had spoken to Audrey and me came to pass. New Life Church became our home church, and Ted Haggard became our pastor, elder, and friend.

We became very involved in the ministry of the church and developed many lifelong relationships that would become integral to the success of our current work. I helped organize some prayer projects in the church. Our third child, Jacob, was born in October of 1993. I started a Royal Ranger outpost, which, after we moved to the mission field, grew to become, for a time, the largest Royal Ranger outpost in the world. During those years we continued to organize prayer for Freedom Ministries and I made trips with David Hogan to Mexico, Australia, and New Zealand.

Our time in Colorado was filled with continued heart refinement and focus. The more I prayed for missionaries, and the more I traveled and attempted to understand the dynamics that come into play in the lives of people who go to a country outside their home culture, who give up being close to their extended families, who leave "normal life," the more I could not really understand.

One day the Lord spoke to me. He essentially said that in order to train missionaries we must become missionaries. I knew that I could gain no more understanding in a way that would be meaningful to them, or us, until we moved outside our small world and followed Him yet again.

Wisdom without understanding leads to misdiagnosis.

Our need to live through the things that other people walk through is not about gaining experience so that we can impart wisdom based upon that experience. It is about gaining understanding by the hand of God so that we can impart wisdom that truly brings life for those we are responsible to serve. Wisdom without understanding leads to misdiagnosis. Selah.

Even Jesus, with all His power and ability, deemed it valuable and necessary to subject Himself to this same dynamic so that we *know* that on all points He has been tempted like us and walked in our shoes.[11] Like Jesus, our ability to empathize with people and their situations comes from walking through similar experiences. Other people's willingness to listen to us often is predicated upon them knowing that we understand their "stuff" because we've "been there."

God can and does speak through anything and anybody, and we should listen to His voice speak through others. Many times Jesus builds disciples who will be able to empathize with others because of a specifically engineered path He has created for them to walk. Sometimes that path is hard.

So after four wonderful years in Colorado, in January of 1996, God sent us forward yet again, this time to Paraguay, a country five thousand miles south of the United States that was totally foreign to us. Audrey was pregnant with our fourth child. Hannah was six, Aspen was four, and Jacob was two. David Pierce, named after his grandfathers, was born while we lived there.

We lived in Paraguay for six months in order to work alongside and encourage a missionary family living there. We faced many difficult/challenging situations: our luggage did not arrive for two weeks; the kids got chicken pox; we got lice; Aspen got an unexplained, ongoing stomach ache; Audrey got a weird rash; we were robbed; our home was invaded by termites; there was an attempted coup; and Audrey had a baby.

Yet our time in Paraguay is a very fond memory for us. Jesus met with us so strongly. Our commitment to pray and worship God together

---

[11] Hebrews 4:14-15

> We saw that our firm conviction to seek God as a family would be the way to feed ourselves spiritually if we were going to thrive at this "missionary thing."

was strengthened. We saw that our firm conviction to seek God as a family would be the way to feed ourselves spiritually if we were going to thrive at this "missionary thing." This was our steadfast anchor.

During our time in Paraguay we had not yet learned Spanish, so we were not super effective as missionaries since we could not communicate with the people. Our main purpose there was to pray for the missionary family and do our best to serve and encourage them. Heaven has recorded whether or not we were effective. They had been serving alone faithfully for years and were close to burnout. We did all we could. And we began to see firsthand the complex dynamics involved in the lives of those who leave home and move to a foreign land to serve God.

We returned to the United States in the summer of 1996 and lived for a year in Woodland Park, Colorado, a mountain town west of Colorado Springs. During that time, David Hogan asked us to commit to full-time work as church planting missionaries with Freedom Ministries. Audrey and I felt hesitation because we knew that God had not called us to just one country. We never heard a specific call to go to Mexico. Our call was to many nations through recruiting, training, placing, and pastoring missionaries all over the world. It was an intimidating and daunting challenge that we were not yet capable of doing. We had prayed for years about working with David Hogan, and now he had asked us directly.

Jesus spoke to me clearly, "Follow David Hogan and you will arrive at what I have called you to do." He had called us to train and place missionaries all around the world. The only information I had concerning that call was what Jesus had told me seven years before on the mountain in the Yellowstone backcountry. I was intimidated and afraid, but I walked forward into the unknown in the face of my fear and doubt.

We met with David Hogan and accepted his invitation to work with him. We made clear that we were not called exclusively to Mexico because of our call to the nations through training missionaries. David responded, "Just give me two years in Mexico, and you can do anything God calls you to do."

As it turned out, those two years turned into twelve. It would have been a disaster had we unhooked in 1999 to attempt to begin training missionaries. I was still lost then, not really knowing Spanish yet, much less having a plan from God for training missionaries.

On the mountain in Yellowstone, God had told me that He would show me how He wanted me to train missionaries. It took me longer than I would have ever dreamed to see what He wanted me to see. In fact, it took me twenty years to understand it clearly, and twelve of those years were spent working with David Hogan in Mexico.

4

The Field Is White

Audrey and I had first experienced Mexico as visitors. I had made a number of trips there alone, but Audrey was anxious to see the field we had prayed for so fervently. She had gone on several short-term mission trips with her family while growing up, so I knew this third-world country would not surprise her. We had been praying for the people of Mexico and our missionary friends for five years, so we were both full of expectation.

In May of 1993, we went to visit the missionaries we had prayed for, for so long. We took our two little girls: Hannah was three and a half and Aspen sixteen months. After we crossed the border into Mexico it took us about ten hours on a bus to reach our destination. I'll let Audrey tell this part of our story.

I was four months pregnant with our third child. It was a very hot afternoon when one of our missionary friends, Jay Williams, drove us in a small, single cab, red Toyota pickup truck to visit a church. All of us—Jay, Britt, our daughters, and I and my belly—squeezed onto the bench seat. The gearshift made it especially hard to find a place to put our legs. It was tight but what an adventure.

We rode along dirt roads lined with simple homes, many of them with thatched grass roofs. The family laundry was hanging on a rope or thrown on a fence or bushes to dry. The sun did its job without any fancy machine. Dogs sunned themselves in the road, often only lifting a head in acknowledgement as we drove by. They seemed not to care that danger from the truck tires was only inches from their head. Chickens, turkeys, and pigs crossed the road at the most untimely moments.

After driving awhile we parked the truck and began to hike. We walked up a small trail, seen only by those who chose to walk there. We came to a fence that we had to cross. As we paused so that each person could crawl through the wires, I remember looking at the lush green mountains surrounding us. I was amazed at the contrast of what I thought Mexico was like and the reality I was seeing.

Always before, my picture of Mexico was of desert wasteland, rocks, cacti, and a sense of barrenness, a place where cowboys plodded along on weary horses in pursuit of a bit of water as they fled the "bad guys," whoever they were.

What I now saw was beautiful. It was as if a green carpet had been rolled out upon the mountains. Green was beside me, in front of me, behind me—green as far as my eyes could see. Flowers bloomed in abundance. A banana plant was at the fence we were about to cross. I stood and captured the picture in my mind. I loved it.

We walked to a house to greet some believers and they offered us something to eat. We sat in their humble home on small simple stools. They served us corn atole in simple bowls. We held it in our hands and carefully watched the missionary to learn how to eat without using any utensils. Hannah and Aspen stood by our side and had their first taste of village food.

We finished with grateful hearts and then went further up the trail. Again, we greeted some believers, and they too invited us to share in their dinner. This house had a toddler who was sitting in a homemade playpen made of sticks. They had stripped the bark and fashioned the sticks into a small rectangular box. It was a simple way to make sure their baby was safe. One of their teenage daughters held Hannah and showed her their animals. She loved it.

Then we went to a church service. The block building had a dirt floor and a few benches. It was simple. Nothing fancy to cause our attention to be on the building itself. It was a useful place to stay out of the sun or rain, a place to gather together and sing and hear the Word of God.

Simple. They had simple homes, simple meals, simple churches, and simple faith.

During that trip Audrey saw, for the first time, where our future was headed. It would not be until November of 1997, four and a half years later, that we would move to the very area we had visited together and begin working as new missionaries. We lived and worked and learned alongside other missionaries and indigenous people in that part of Mexico for six years before we were sent out in 2003 to start working from scratch.

Submission

Our move to the new area of ministry in 2003 was the first move like that I'd ever made, where I did not hear the original instruction directly from God myself. Our leader, David Hogan, sent us out. I was given the choice of where to go—all I needed to do was find an area where there were indigenous people who did not know Jesus, with enough room to work for many years.

Honestly, I did not like the idea very much to start with, but Jesus had told me to follow David Hogan and that in time He would lead me to what He had called me to do. It wasn't a matter of how much I liked it. This was a part of my training process. We learn important spiritual things from each other. In fact, we are commanded to teach others to obey Jesus.[12]

Submission is essential in following Jesus, because, like Jesus, we learn obedience through the things we suffer.[13] Submission is learned by submitting to one another. Just talking about submission isn't enough, because submission is not an issue until we are asked to do things we don't like or agree with. Only then do we discover where we really stand related to submission.

I am not talking about the wrong kind of submission, for example, being asked to do something that is sinful. We should never submit to sin, no matter who is involved.

When Jesus assigns you to follow a leader, I believe it has everything to do with what He wants to do in you and little to do with the person He assigns you to follow. So many who are called to follow leaders for a time get distracted and derailed by trying to change the human flaws about the leader they are following—instead of focusing on their own life and what Jesus is doing in them.

I now know that the reason I did not like the idea of going and start-ing a work from scratch was that I was afraid I did not have the qualities God expected me to have to succeed in birthing a network of churches, not just one church. I hid that fear behind the fact that I, personally, had not gotten the idea directly from God. So God had to push me, through my leader, the very man that Jesus *had* told me to follow.

---

[12] Matthew 28:18-20 *v. 20

[13] Hebrews 5:8

When I sat down in the middle of my turbulence to ask God what was up, because I was about to have a serious conflict with my leader over this, God said to me, "Don't be afraid to go in the direction you have been pointed." That ended my unsettledness and any desire to resist being told to make this major move. I began to get excited, all the while still experiencing serious doubt and fear. So Audrey and I prayed and put action to our prayers.

It turned out to be one of the best decisions I ever made.

I left in my truck with my coworker, Tim Funte, who had been given the same assignment for his family. We scouted in the direction where we had been pointed, an area as wide as the country of Mexico and as long as approximately half its length. Over the course of ten days we drove for twenty-five hundred miles, looking and praying, shooting completely in the dark.

I drove miles and miles of pavement, following a tugging in my spirit about where to turn and what mountains to drive into. As I drove I would sense a pull toward an area or mountain range. I would get to a range, and that pull would keep me moving forward over more mountains and through huge valleys, first turning here, and then there, until I drove through the remote town that would eventually become our home. When I drove into that town, I felt God prick my heart.

I returned to get my family. We loaded up a few days later and returned—this time by a more direct route—to the place of the

> Courage is not the absence of fear, but right action in the face of the fear that you have.

pricking. God spoke to Audrey and the kids, too. We all knew this was it, so we moved. We left all the structure of the mature and awesome work we had been a part of (seasoned missionaries, mature national pastors, and about three hundred churches)—and were sent out to start one ourselves.

I knew this was the right thing, so I had to move forward in spite of my fear, in spite of my doubt and inexperience, and in spite of the fact that I was moving my family to a new and unknown area. We would be alone and therefore more vulnerable. However, I knew that "He who is with us is greater"—greater than everything.

Jesus likes faith and courage. The Bible says in Revelation 21:8 that cowards go to hell. I did not want to be a coward, so I faced my fear and we moved. A coward is not someone who is afraid, but someone who allows their fear to keep them from moving forward in what God has called them to do. Courage is not the absence of fear, but right action in the face of the fear that you have.

If there is no true risk, then there is no true substance when victory proves triumphant and produces the awesome testimony of the living Christ.

I have been brought many times in my life to the confluence of hope and fear. I think that without arriving at this most unsettlingly desirable spot, faith cannot exercise itself. Without true risk, faith is not engaged to produce anything but the ordinary.

Without true risk, faith is not engaged to produce anything but the ordinary.

As I said before, we sought God every morning in our house, praying for direction, and one day Jesus said, "*Live according to the pattern I have given you: pray, fast, and worship mostly. And when you leave your house you will watch Me work."*

Not long after He said that to me, the first person got saved, affectionately known to our family as "Armadillo Man." That was in late July of 2003. Since then, I have been drawn down a road of His choosing, pulled forward by a powerful vacuum, a vacuum of the work of the Holy Spirit. A vacuum that is void of foreign elements and draws everything to Himself. Souls saved. Healing. Deliverance. The presence of God. All orchestrated by the Holy Spirit, and not by my experience. I stepped out of my door and was amazed at the work He was doing. It took all of my training, all my education, all my gifts, all my talents, and all of the anointing He had given me just to respond to what He was doing. I stayed amazed at what I saw occurring all around me. As we followed the work of the Holy Spirit in the lives of people, we saw the evidence that as we stayed out of His way, flowed with Him, and did not hinder His work with man-inspired ideas—extraordinary things happened.

It's easier, I think, to find a systematic pattern for church planting and growth and follow that. The problem with that method, though, is it has too much man thinking involved in it. It leans too much on man's experience and good intentions, rather than on Christ alone. When we mix the wisdom of man with the wisdom of God, we empty the Cross of its power.

If we are not continually working toward complete surrender, then we can have no surety that Jesus will move in power. If we lay down our life and fight every day to keep it down, then extraordinary things begin to occur. I do not always win the wrestling match with my own life, but I am committed to the fight to surrender until I die. And once I die, to stay dead.

5

The Presence

Ever since I was young, wandering in the woods near my home, I hungered for more of the presence of God. I had experienced the closeness of God on many occasions, but on the mission field I was about to encounter Him in a whole new, mind-blowing way.

In February of 1998, only about two and a half months after we had moved to Mexico, there was a pastors' conference that was to last three days. About five hundred pastors and leaders, mostly men, gathered. Each day started at 6 a.m. with early morning prayer. Then the service continued all day and into the night with alternating prayer, worship, preaching, and more worship.

On the second day, around 3:30 a.m., Audrey and I woke up our small children, aged twenty-one months, four, six, and eight, and drove two hours to church. I led prayer that morning and found the presence of God more tangible and intense than I had ever experienced in my entire life. His presence seized me and it literally felt like fire. Jeremiah described this in Jeremiah 20:9, but unlike Jeremiah, I did not feel like a fire was shut up in my bones. Instead, it felt like the fire came from my bones and saturated my entire being, ready to break out and also burn all who were around me.

The day became a blur.

At about 6:30 p.m. our leaders asked for volunteers to stay at least another two hours while most of the missionaries and visitors returned home. I was worn to a frazzle from worshiping with all my might for two days, and I wanted to go home and take a shower and rest like everybody else. But I'd been taught growing up that you step up and serve when there is a need. So I volunteered to stay. Our emotions are so deceitful and weak. Had I listened to my feelings and gone home, I would have missed an experience with God that I treasure to my deepest core.

A coworker took Audrey and the kids home. For them too, it was the end of a long day. Little did I know what was shortly to take place or I never would have sent my family home! They would gladly have welcomed being more exhausted and hot in order to experience the theophany that occurred.

As the service continued that evening I stood up on a small bank on the edge of the crowd merely observing. Honestly, I was so tired I was not participating that much in the service. About twenty minutes after the other missionaries and my family left, I noticed something unusual happening. The believers were worshiping God with wild abandon, as they had off and on for the last twelve hours, when I heard an unusual sound I'd never heard before. It was one sound, but forged by many voices in a harmonic unison, coming from the throats of most of the men. The sound captured the full attention of my spirit. It was so astounding, so wonderful, that my mouth dropped open in amazement, and I thought—*This must be the kind of sound that destroyed the walls of Jericho!*

I've never heard anything like it in worship before or since. It seemed like I could almost see the sound wave coming from the throats of hundreds of pastors and leaders.

I wonder what other wonders like this Heaven has in store for us?

As the sound captivated all of my mind, emotions, and desires, with my whole being focused upon God, I saw something unique and unexpected. Our team had erected two 30 x 60 foot blue tarps for a sunshade, and even though the sun had set and the moon was rising, all the believers were packed in under this provisional roof. Toward the front of the crowd, six of the ten indigenous elders of our movement were dancing in cadence with the rhythm and waves of the sound caused by the voices of the people.

With their eyes closed, the men seemed propelled by a power beyond themselves. They flowed in harmony within a circle about fifteen yards in diameter—all of them moving in elliptical orbits around each other, never bumping or touching the other or the crowd that formed the outer perimeter of their ring. I stood in awe and felt the magnetic drawing of God.

I decided I wanted to join in the circle with these men. The pull of this was irresistible. I made my way around to the back of the crowd and there saw another one of the ten elders praying for individuals in the crowd, so I joined him and we prayed together for person after person, slowly working our way to the front while the people continued to worship.

The crowd was tightly packed, the attention of all the people riveted upon God. As I continued interceding in prayer, I tried to weave my way through the crowd, always aware that I was being pulled by the overwhelming presence of God toward that circle of men up front.

I felt the fire of God surging through me, and as I prayed and slowly moved forward, I saw the power of the Holy Spirit run ahead of me like a wave breaking on the beach that knocked over about seventy-five people. In less than ten seconds, a passageway about four feet wide opened before me, through the tightly packed crowd, all the way to the front. The ground was covered with a tangle of bodies that the power of God had just tumbled.

I began to make my way down that opening toward the six elders. Those elders were still orbiting each other in concentric patterns, ever changing but precisely mathematical in their geometrical movements.

After I had moved halfway to the front of the outdoor church, suddenly a force knocked me face down to the ground wedged between bodies already there. As I pitched forward I felt the most intense sense of my own wickedness I'd ever experienced. The conviction was palpable and overwhelming. The depths of my own sinfulness pierced through my soul.

I began to sob, deep wails ripping from my chest and tears spilling from my eyes. I felt that I was approaching something holy but I was desperately unclean. My body was wracked with sorrow, and my repentance was squeezing and twisting out of me a grudging recognition of my carnality. I was pinned to the ground by the crushing weight of my sinfulness. Even though I tried I could not rise.

I lost track of time and many minutes passed—maybe almost an hour—before at last I felt squeezed out. The weight lifted and I felt light, like a vapor of fire. I sat up on my knees. I looked at my arms, expecting to see flames, but none were visible.

I stood up, still feeling the fire, still being pulled as if by a magnet toward the moving column of worship. The sound was as powerful as ever, undiminished by time or any fatigue of the worshipers. The hand of God was moving His people.

I now sensed I could move past my spot of repentance, nearer to the presence of God. Ahead of me about thirty feet away, I saw another elder—not in the circle with the others—barely able to hold himself erect while grasping a podium. In my hand I held a bandana, which I used as a napkin to wipe my mouth when sharing a meal with the people. I felt the power of God boiling in me! I impulsively felt the urge to pop my bandana at him, like you would if you were having a towel fight with your friends, even though I was thirty feet away from him. I have no idea why I did this. It just felt right.

The elder was looking down, his head hunched between his shoulders, his hands on the table with elbows locked, attempting to hold himself off the ground because the glory of God was pushing down on him. One meaning of the word "glory" means weight. When God chooses to move like this, sometimes His glory becomes a tangible weight that can push you to the ground. I have experienced this many times. When I popped my bandana in his direction, an unseen, but obvious wave of power hit that brother, knocking him through the air, back and upward toward the outside wall of the small church building next to this temporary shelter we'd erected.

This mysterious power of God had moved the man backward, up off his feet, and then pinned him to the wall of the church with his feet four feet off the ground! He remained suspended there for at least thirty seconds. Then he fell to the ground in a heap, out of my sight, and I did not see what happened to him next.

I continued unhindered to the front, stepping through the tangle of people that the power of the Holy Spirit had knocked down over half an hour before. Finally, I was able to step into the moving circle of elders, and the flowing amalgam of God's presence seized me also. I was pulled in, moved, and quickly synchronized with the other six men—closing my eyes like the others.

It was something I'd not experienced before and haven't since. It was wonderful and exhilarating. Time seemed suspended and I had no fear or worry. I did not tire. All I can say is that it was some type of different dimension, a convergence of the supernatural and the natural, but I remained cognizant of the "here and now."

I opened my eyes, wondering if I was going to hit any of the other brothers or if they were going to crash into me, but we never collided. Some of the men had their arms spread wide and their heads back. We were all caught up in the actual presence of our Father! Nothing else mattered.

In time the flow let me loose to stand alone in the exact center of the rotating circle. I opened my eyes and saw the tarps above me flapping in the breeze. The spot where they overlapped had separated, and when the breeze opened a gap, I saw the moon. It was very dry at that time and all of the shuffling feet had created a three-inch thick layer of baby powder fine dust under the blue tarps. Our dancing feet had stirred up motes of dust that were forming a cloud above us into a column the exact diameter of the circle of us dancing men. The column of dust looked like a pillar twenty feet high. The dust, in effect, showed a visible sign of the swirling motion of the presence that was moving and consuming us.

I stood in awe, wishing so strongly that all the others who had gone home could witness this miracle too. I remember thinking, *Where is everybody? Where are all of the missionaries, and why were they not here to see this? Where are my wife and kids? My mother? My dad? My brother? My sisters? My dearest friends? They should all be here. This is indescribably wonderful!*

As I stood in amazement inside the circle, I began to focus more carefully on the dust. The color of the dust particles forming the pillar began to change from a grey-brown to a brilliant golden-white. The molecules of the air took on this brighter color, and the swirling pattern grew more visible. This brilliance was so striking that other aspects of my surroundings faded into obscurity.

The sound coming from the people was still strong, but the glory I was now observing took precedence over everything. I looked down, and it seemed that the ground beneath me had disappeared. I looked up and it seemed that the tarp, too, was no longer visible and even the people near me seemed to have disappeared. I believe now that I was standing in the middle of a pillar of the glory of God with six men and myself caught up in its circulation.

I wonder if it was something like this that kept the Egyptians at bay so long ago when the Jews were making their escape? Heaven has marvels that are beyond our comprehension, so why would we be surprised by a manifestation like this? What I do know is that in that simple shelter, for many hours, people who loved God and believed that He was who He said He was, had been worshiping their hearts out!

The measure of good worship is not how good the music is or the talent or anointing of the band. Nor is the measure how the people respond. The measure of good worship is how God responds.

> The measure of good worship is not how good the music is or the talent or anointing of the band. Nor is the measure how the people respond. The measure of good worship is how God responds.

It is the presence of God that has so impacted my life. It is this presence that I want others to enjoy. The presence is all about fellowship with Him. If I cannot find a way to transfer this understanding, then I will believe my life in a significant way is a failure.

I am not living to teach doctrine. I am living to introduce people to Jesus, and convince them to seek Him with all their heart, with all their mind, with all their soul, and with all their strength. Jesus died a sacrificial death so that we can have a vibrant, visceral relationship with Him and His father. I think that to replace that with anything else is to demean the death of the Son of God.

Nothing can compare to experiencing the presence of God!

6

Family

My wife, Audrey, and I have determined that ministry is not something we *do* but it is who we *are*. We don't go witnessing—we *are* witnesses. Ministry is not my job or career. I am an ambassador of the Kingdom of God. So is every other member of our family. This is our family purpose.

Our ministry does not steal our life or compete with family. This *is* our life. This *is* our family. We have endeavored to give our children ownership in the work that we do. We have all laid down our lives for the sake of advancing the Kingdom of God.

Jesus is brilliant with His plans for mankind, and the family is His destined platform to give us, and the world, the preview for His Kingdom. It is the pattern that we are supposed to follow in planting and growing churches. This cannot be taught in seminars or absorbed from social engineering. It must be *worked out* as life progresses, infused with the value that Jesus lives and breathes life into those who trust Him.

Family *does* work when Jesus is allowed to fill the progression of living and growing with His Presence

Our family's life does not revolve around our kids' activities, my career, or any other activity or purpose. All of these things, many of them quite wonderful in their own right, are what so easily distract many families in the Kingdom of God. I stay puzzled by the fact that so many Christian parents just live life and somehow seem to believe that their high calling is merely to raise good moral kids, help them get a college education, marry the right person, get established in a career, provide for their family, and generally contribute to society in a positive way.

I think the purpose of such families is out of focus. Often there is only passive Kingdom focus, not much energy for the Gospel, and the practical, pragmatic things of this temporal life dominate their time, resources, life philosophy, and worldview.

> I believe the family is God's first institution and is the strongest unit of ministry that exists on this planet. Kingdom purpose should be the thing that defines our family.

I believe the family is God's first institution and is the strongest unit of ministry that exists on this planet. Kingdom purpose should be the thing that defines our family.

Oh, how awesome is the power of a family who advances the Gospel together. Ask any one of my children and you will see that they have identified with the work God has us doing. Have they suffered with us? Yes. Have they made the work more difficult from a practical standpoint? Yes. Are we more vulnerable to danger? Yes. Is it more expensive with them along? Yes. Would I, or any one of them, change the way they have been raised and what they have been a part of and seen? Unequivocally no!

Ultimately, my children will make their own decisions of whether or not they continue in their adult years to work in the calling that Jesus has given us now. Jesus will brand them as He sees fit. Audrey and I have always told them that we will not tell them God's will for their lives; that is something they must find out on their own. We will support them in whatever God is telling them to do. They do not have to be "full-time" ministers to fulfill God's purpose for their lives. We are all called to be full-time ministers of the Gospel regardless of what our occupation is. We must bring the truth of the Gospel to people in every walk of life and in every sphere of influence.

———

Audrey does not strive with me for her "own" ministry. She is strong and capable herself on any level, but she has chosen to run together with me in this three-legged race we call our life. She is brimming with talent and ability. Academically, she graduated first in her class in the school of education at Auburn University.

Audrey was raised in the home of a pediatrician in Atlanta, Georgia. She had no lack of the material things of this life, yet I have never seen any selfishness in her attitude or expectations. Her parents did an amazing job raising this woman who is my rib. She is athletic, beautiful, and loves Jesus with all of her being. She is full of gifts, the most evangelistic person I have ever met, prophetic, and intensely nurturing. She can hold a conversation with the young and old, the brilliant and the simple. She is the most honest person I know, truly noble and strong as her name "Audrey" means. She could "be" anything or anybody she wanted to be.

But Audrey chose to be my wife, and there is order for life lived together as one. I have never dragged her anywhere. She runs with me. We work seamlessly together in the life we lead. Her life has always been full: taking care of me, teaching our children school, and responding to the ministry that simply living life positions her for. She has led many people to Jesus as she, along with the rest of us, does her best to seize the opportunities at hand.

In all the difficult and dark things we have lived in and walked through, she has been the most steadfast and eternally conscious person I have ever met. Her ability to adjust to foreign environments is demonstrated in her life as she merely assesses whether or not Jesus is taking us somewhere. If the answer is yes, then there is nothing she won't adjust to. She just goes and makes life better for everyone who is with us.

Audrey has maintained a living sanctuary for our children and me in the midst of extreme stress. She makes the environment around her beautiful, and is steadfast and unmoving. We truly are one, and we have never had a whole day with a disruption in our harmony.

I have a living miracle! Those who know us can testify that she, more than anyone else, is the stability that keeps me moving forward. She has impacted my life so. To know her has given me inexhaustible fuel to become the man I should be, because she is Audrey, the greatest gift God has placed in my life.

We do what we do together. Each family member plays an important part in bringing the Gospel to these pagan people. How would our children know what a marriage is under God if they don't observe ours? How can they understand what it means to live in the presence of God if they don't see it in us?

Discipleship doesn't happen with just good literature or programs. Disciples are made by other disciples. Our kids need to see the example of what God wants for them lived out by Audrey and me.

If you, in your family, are building a house of cards, influenced by your culture and the values of the surrounding society, then your house will surely fall when adversity knocks on the door.

It is our responsibility as parents to train up our children. This means that we should teach them the Bible, lead them into praying, and offer them the environment where they can experience the presence of God. I will not abdicate that responsibility to any pastor or other person, regardless of how wonderful they might be. This is what Jesus wants parents to do!

Our kids have seen God do dramatic things. They have been ministering their whole lives in the work Jesus has us doing. All of what we do is for Him; therefore the ministry has stolen nothing from them. I wish that all believers could have their children witness the things our kids have seen with their own eyes.

As we seek God and worship Him daily as a family, we move through the day encountering the awesome works that God is doing among us. I never know what I will encounter as I make my way from village to village. Likewise, I never know what God will bring to our home while I am gone.

One day, as I was gone attending to business in the city, a lady came to our house with her son. Audrey will relate what she and the children saw happen.

The children and I were doing school upstairs in our home in Mexico when someone rang the doorbell. I went down to see who it was. At the door was a lady dressed in traditional indigenous clothes and a young teenage boy. She said the boy was her thirteen-year-old son and he had hurt his arm. They wanted prayer. I invited them in so I could hear their story and then pray.

Once inside she told me that earlier that morning while she was washing dishes, she had sent her son to collect firewood for cooking. She had heard him cry out in pain. She was alarmed because she knew that was unusual—he was a typical, tough young boy who wouldn't want to show his pain. She went outside to check on him. He had fallen down and hit his arm on a "stob," a small tree sapling cut close to the ground with a machete, the small stump creating a very sharp point.

This mother had wrapped her son's arm in a big sling and brought him to town so that they could go to the clinic, but had decided to stop by our house first for prayer. She told me she had come by before and that Jesus had answered our prayers. She had faith that Jesus would respond again.

I thought that since he had landed on a sharp point that maybe his arm was cut open and bloody. Maybe I could clean and bandage the wound.

"May I look at his arm?" I asked.

The momma carefully unwrapped the sling. Immediately the boy began to favor his arm, and hold it close to his body. I saw that it was not bleeding but severely bent at the wrong place. Instead of his hand bending from his wrist, it bent further up his arm, about two inches above his wrist bone. There was a bump there, and though I'm not a nurse, I felt I was looking at a broken arm. I told the mom to wrap the arm back up in the sling. The boy was in obvious pain.

I went upstairs to get the kids and our housekeeper to join me in prayer. I told them what was going on and asked them to come pray with me. We all went downstairs and the momma wanted to show them his arm. He hesitantly pulled the sling back a bit and they all saw the same bump and unnatural angle of his arm. Knots formed at his jaw as he clinched his teeth, fighting to keep from crying out.

We began to pray. His mother went to her knees and began to pray in her native Nahuatl. The rest of us prayed in Spanish and English. When I ran out of Spanish vocabulary, I continued in English. When I could no longer express the cry of my heart in words at all, I began to pray in tongues. We all cried out to God for about ten minutes and felt the Holy Spirit fill the room. Our desperate cries turned to calm.

When we stopped I asked the boy how he felt. He said it still hurt, but he began to move the arm around a bit. He winced some but moved his arm more. Then he began to stretch his arm out, the bump disappeared, and his arm straightened. God had painlessly set his broken bone in front of our eyes. We couldn't believe it...yet it was happening! The boy rotated his arm and stretched it out again. He smiled! This time it was perfectly normal!

His momma gasped and fell to her knees in front of him. She began to move his arm and twist and turn it. He was still a bit sore, but healed! She began to wail in gratitude to our Lord and buried her face in her lace huipil. I began to cry as well. A miracle. We had just seen a miracle. We were so thankful.

I spoke to the boy about how Jesus has a purpose and plan for him and that he should walk with Him all the days of his life. They left happy. We all were amazed and blessed.

How is it that the mom knew where she could get help? It is because the Gospel that we preach is not just heard, it is also seen. The opportunity for the unsaved to *see* God move is 50 percent of the Gospel we "preach." The Spirit's power is shown so that people who are hopeless have a reason to hope. The people we reach out to have no fluff in their lives. All of their talents, all of their effort, and all of their resources are used just to stay alive. Information has little value to them.

Some say that Holy Spirit power is now only for the heart-level things, the intellectual things, the Christianized things. But we say, based on the Word of God and what we experience on a daily basis, that Jesus has not changed, nor will He change. He is the same. The things that He did when He walked this earth are the things that He does today and will continue to do, no matter how much theological education tries to render His power merely historical.[14]

This is the reality that we live...as a family.

[14] Hebrews 13:8

7

Opposition

The enemy is at work in Mexico, the same as he is in all lands. You may ask, "What about all those mountain areas where the Gospel has not been heard?" We have encountered a deep darkness there, a darkness that had never been penetrated with Light. Satan's been enslaving and blinding people there for centuries. He never will give up until God commands that he be bound and cast into the pit.

I learned soon after moving to Mexico that true spiritual warfare was different from what I'd previously thought and taught. Much of what I had learned in the States did not seem to work the way I thought it did in a part of the world where principalities had never been challenged with the victory of the Lord Jesus on the Cross. It's a demonic darkness trapping nearly 14 million indigenous people, and over 90 million Mexicans in the bondage of hell. The indigenous people we work with are difficult to get to and then hard to minister to. And once reached they are even harder to maintain in their faith.

A visitor from the States came to visit us in our second year on the field. He noted how tired and rundown I looked. He listened to the testimonies and the description of the "spiritual environment" around us. His desire to encourage and help me led him to say, "Well, brother, have you prayer-walked your neighborhood? Have you prayer-walked those villages and torn down the high places controlling them?"

I looked at him in disbelief. It was his first day there, so he didn't know yet that we did all of that regularly! But the spiritual opposition was intense! By the end of his visit a week later, he was worn to a frazzle, had developed a nervous twitch, and was in an obvious hurry to leave. It seemed that he'd had his first real-world encounter with darkness. He experienced what we live with constantly, that just because you let the vocabulary word "Jesus" pass your teeth does not mean anything to the enemy in his well-established domain. The name of Jesus *is* all-powerful and every authority has to bow, but the enemy is interested in whether or not we will stay the course and see to it that souls are rescued. In other words, the devil refuses to flee without a fight.

In my experience, if we travel somewhere and attempt to seize control of the spiritual climate but do not work to get people saved and discipled, we have not even gotten the devil's attention.

> The name of Jesus *is* all-powerful and every authority has to bow, but the enemy is interested in whether or not we will stay the course and see to it that souls are rescued. In other words, the devil refuses to flee without a fight.

I am convinced that "strategic level prayer" cannot *occupy and take territory* for the Master. To use a military metaphor, there needs to be "boots on the ground."

Strategic prayer is like the air power of the Air Force that immensely helps those of us on the ground to rescue souls. We desperately need all the prayer cover we can get! Prayer is the nerve impulse that moves the hand of God, and it can be done from any location on earth. Prayer helps us to see the kingdom of darkness rendered powerless in the lives of people, but it does not in itself bind the devil.

If we successfully change the spiritual climate of a region by spiritual warfare through prayer and intercession—and we certainly have the authority in Jesus' name to do that—but people living there still go to hell, what's the point? The most strategic battlefield in this spiritual war we are fighting is the battlefield inside people's hearts and minds. The climate around them is secondary. For the people who will spend eternity in hell, the kingdom of darkness was not bound! The only thing that truly binds the devil is when people give their hearts to Jesus and live that decision out for the rest of their lives. That happens in places where the spiritual climate is very open and easy, and that happens in places where the spiritual climate is very closed and difficult.

To try to engage the enemy without prayer, worship, intercession, self-discipline, and action to seek and save the lost is disastrous. If we do not pray, we will not stay.

I learned the intensity of our opposition fairly early after moving to Mexico. I departed our house one morning with Beau Barton. He and his new wife, Rachel, were visiting us, investigating the possibility of becoming missionaries. We drove to a rendezvous point three hours away where we'd meet two other missionaries, Shawn Williamson and Tim Funte. After we arrived, the three of us joined Shawn in his truck and rode three more hours high up into the mountains where three services were scheduled.

Upon arriving at the first location, I stepped out of the front seat of the truck. As I shut the door and walked toward a spectacular overlook, I felt an invisible wave wash over me, starting at the top my head and moving down my body to my feet. I knew this was a bad thing and felt it was witchcraft. Mexico is saturated with the black arts, and the farther back in the mountains you go, the worse it gets.

The villagers in this area lived in terror because many of them had seen the manifestation of a demon spirit that was catalyzed by black magic warlocks who were known to offer human sacrifices. The people told us of pits hidden in the mountains that they believed were openings to hell. The local people called this demon spirit the "father of the mountain." When I stepped out of the truck I met this principality.

Immediately I began to experience what felt like severe flu symptoms. The color drained from my face and I felt dizzy. We walked to the hut where we would hold the first service, but with every step I took I felt drawn into a tunnel of weakness and pain, my every bone aching and muscles not wanting to respond. A spiraling delirium wove itself into my thought processes, and my resolve began to fail.

All this happened within two minutes after I stepped out of the truck and was confronted by the kingdom of darkness that had control of the people we were there to rescue.

I weakly made it through the first service. The four of us returned to the truck to begin our drive to the next village where we would have our second service. I climbed into the truck and instantly fell into a fitful, almost delirious sleep. In my family I was raised not to complain, so I said nothing to my coworkers. They just thought I was feeling bad and was sleeping.

I was awakened when we arrived at the next village. It was my turn to preach there and somehow I was strengthened enough to deliver the message I had prepared.

The sustenance I felt, however, was temporary and as soon as we were done with that service and got back in the truck, I went out again.

The third service was cancelled for some reason I cannot recall, and so we returned to where we had met up that morning. My friends shook me awake, and all I could think of was getting home to Audrey.

Beau and I got in my truck and took off for home. We had two-way radios in all of our trucks and houses so we could communicate truck to truck and house to truck over long distances. The mountains interfere with signal transmission so we had learned where the call spot windows were. When I started driving I immediately began to call Audrey, who was at our house, but where we were was not a good radio call spot. I knew that the closest call spot was at least an hour's drive, but I kept calling anyway, my mind spinning in a fever-induced, near delirium.

For the whole three-hour trip home, I called every few minutes but most attempts never connected. I remember very little of the drive that night nor how I found myself in one piece, parked in front of our house.

Audrey came outside when I pulled up, and when I opened my door I fell out of the cab into her arms. She had answered me the few times she heard me call, but that was lost in a deep fog of my memory. She had realized that something was terribly wrong with me because of the way I answered her and sometimes babbled incoherently on the radio. She had been waiting anxiously, knowing my progress coming home by my constant calling on the radio. Beau picked me up and carried me into the house and placed me on the couch. Then they decided to move me to my bed.

In alarm, Audrey pulled everyone together to call out to God to touch me. My whole family and Beau and Rachel were gathered around the bed, earnestly praying. I continued to babble, not making any sense. Then, suddenly, I couldn't draw in a breath. I struggled, unable to breathe, and then all went dark. No one recalls exactly how long I was not breathing. It was about a minute or so. Then I came to, suddenly gasping! It was then that I saw everyone, with a clear head. Thank God for a family that knows in a desperate situation to call on God with a whole heart first!

My mind had cleared, but I felt like I had a dozen mud holes stomped into my body! My family's prayers had brought me back that night.

As I've said earlier, from young to old, our children know Jesus and how to access His power.

The next morning I was super weak and could not get out of bed, but I was able to rest calmly with a clear mind. Beau and Rachel were flying back to the United States early the following morning so we needed to drive them the two hours to the city that afternoon. We wanted to be sure and get them close to the airport so they could easily get to the airport in the early morning on the day of their flight. I was so weak Audrey had to drive. We checked into a hotel and I collapsed on the bed and immediately fell asleep.

The next morning I felt a little stronger and took them to the airport, only a ten-minute drive. By the time I got back to the hotel, however, I was exhausted and fell into bed for another five hours of sleep. We then checked out and Audrey drove us home.

The next day I had three services scheduled, two of them requiring strenuous hikes in the mountainous terrain. In the morning I felt stronger and was able to walk from the bedroom to the living room without passing out! The policy of our mission is to avoid missing a service or appointment at almost any cost. If you can get up and walk to your truck, then you must keep your word and go do ministry. We know that the devil will pull any trick to stop us from rescuing people from hell, so we go. This is what we give our lives for.

However, this particular day I wondered if I could make the scheduled hikes. In fact, I wasn't sure I could even drive to the rendezvous point and meet the other missionaries so we could go on together. I said goodbye to Audrey and the kids, they prayed for me as they always did when I left, I got into my truck, and drove to the first call spot where I could contact Jo-D Hogan, whom I was meeting that morning. I called him on the radio and told him what had transpired over the last couple of days. He told me to come on and meet him, and he would carry me if necessary. "But don't give into the enemy!" he exhorted. So with a weary sigh I drove on.

Two hours later I arrived at Jo-D's, who was in charge for the day. In addition to him, there were two other missionaries who were going with us as well. We got in Jo-D's truck and drove to where we needed to park, about a forty-five minute trip.

It was a very hot day, about 115 degrees Fahrenheit. We were going to hike two and a half miles up a mountain, gaining at least one thousand feet in elevation. The first mile the trail was quite flat, but I still was really dragging, just clenching my teeth and putting one foot in front of the other. I refused to even think of the almost straight-up mountain ahead. At the point where the trail started the steep incline, we stopped at a freshwater spring and stood in the shade, mainly for my benefit.

After the brief rest we started hiking up, and I felt so weak that I thought I might pass out. I grabbed ahold of Jo-D's backpack. He's as strong as a mule and he began pulling me up the mountain. I could only make a few steps at a time and my heart was beating so hard I thought it was going to beat out of my chest as I gasped for breath. My eyes were slits of determination as I was dragged up the mountainside. I have lost count of the mountains I have climbed in my life, but none was ever so difficult.

Approximately halfway up the mountainside, I felt something wash over my entire body—another wave, like the evil one I'd felt before. But this time it was different—it was a touch of Heaven! Power filled my legs and arms and back. Air filled my lungs, and I stood up straight. I wanted to run!

"Let's go!" I said to my coworkers. They rejoiced at seeing, yet again, Heaven touch earth! We went up that mountain and preached the Gospel.

The Spirit of God had come upon me on that mountainside and healed me. He had healed me in the going!

> The Spirit of God had come upon me on that mountainside and healed me. He had healed me in the going!

Ultimately, I believe that this is the focus of spiritual warfare—the souls of men.

Our family and missionary team pray earnestly almost every day and for extended seasons we fast every other day. We read and study the Bible constantly. We worship God passionately in our home and in our services. We live in constant confrontation with the forces of darkness, but if our intercession was not followed by ground-level engagement for souls by us or someone else, I think our efforts would be no more effective than spitting in the wind. When we fast and pray and intercede, we have not finished anything. The fight is not finished; it's just started.

8

In the Face of Doubt

In January of 2003, before we moved to begin a work from scratch, I was ministering in a village a good five-hour drive from my home. I had just finished with the service for that night, and while I was waiting for the believers I had hauled from other villages to climb into the back of my truck for the ride home, we heard the sound of a motorcycle coming down the dirt road that led to the village.

The Honda XR 600R dirt bikes we used have a distinctive sound, and our missionaries were the only ones riding these bikes in that part of Mexico. It was never a good sign when a missionary came to a make an unscheduled visit to a village.

My heart sank. I knew he was coming to tell me that my sister, Kathy, had died.

My friend and coworker, Jay Williams, stepped off his motorcycle and looked at me. I knew. I collapsed in the mud puddle at my feet. Not because my sister had made it to Heaven, for that is *the* point, but because I felt I had failed to see my sister healed. Throughout our life and ministry we had seen countless miracles and healings. We had also experienced many people who did not get healed, but that did not dampen my sense of loss, grief, and failure.

For twelve years we had prayed, fasted, and sought God for Kathy's healing—only now to do a funeral? Something inside me shriveled up. The hope that I had the anointing, or the faith, or whatever it is that causes the hand of God to move and fix these kinds of things fled my heart.

My sister was dead, killed by cancer. All I could do was lie down in the mud and weep.

I had laid hands on thousands of people and seen many miracles touch every kind of problem. Over the history of the ministry that I worked with in Mexico, there had been many people raised from the dead throughout hundreds of villages. Every type of miracle and healing that can be found in the Bible was happening around us all the time. Healing power was normal and frequent throughout a broad system of local churches.

But now that my sister had died, I wilted inside, deep in my subconscious. The threat of the enemy convinced me that I just did not have what it took to see God deal with complicated diseases. The ability to confront other types of problems was not affected in my heart. But cancer—this disease had killed my sister, and nothing I could do could alter that.

I'm not a person who easily gives up. My dad had always found a way around problems. "Cain't never did nuthin'," he'd said to me so often it was branded on my brain tissue. This was different—I had never hit a dead stop inside me before.

When Kathy died my will to fight for healings of cancer died also. This response was contrary to what the Bible teaches. It was contrary to my training. It was contrary to my experience. It was contrary to who I was raised to be. *Hancocks do not give up.* But I did that night.

Lying in muddy water, miles up a dirt road, in the dark, far from home, I did not give up on life, or ministry, or miracles, or on the power of God. I just gave up on seeing cancer healed. Doubt in this area wrestled its way on top of my faith and pinned it down.

———

A year after Kathy's death, and seven months after moving to pioneer a new area, I was brought to the hut of a sick man by Tino, one of the first people who had been saved after we'd arrived in those mountains. He told me his cousin, Roberto, was dying and wanted us to come to his house. This is how the Gospel spreads in our work. There must be a reason for these people to ask for help. That reason is the power of God. We had seen many people healed, and those testimonies had made their way to this sick man.

We hiked through the jungle and down the side of a canyon to a small house hidden among the plant life. We were invited in and sat down in the dim interior. There was no electricity in this hut. No running water. The floor was dirt. Their stove was a fire made on a raised dirt platform.

Roberto weakly pulled himself up off of his bed of boards and sat in a cracked, blue plastic chair, and we began to hear his story. He was very thin and had difficulty talking, barely able to form words with his mouth. Roberto said he had lost about twenty kilos (forty-four pounds) in the previous nine days. He had not eaten anything solid for three months, and had consumed only water, a spoonful at a time, in the past week.

The more my eyes adjusted to the dim light and the more I heard, a dread and sorrow grew inside me. During his narrative I asked Roberto if he had been to see any doctors. He said yes, so I asked what they called his problem. "They told me I have throat cancer," he said, "and that I have to get an operation. The operation costs $25,000 pesos. We do not have the money, so they sent me home and told me that I was going to die."

Roberto was spending his final days on a bed made of boards, crying without hope, because he was wasting away in terrible pain. And his wife and a little daughter were going to lose their husband and father. I had noticed by now that the left side of his neck was grossly swollen from the base of his skull down into his shoulder.

I was overwhelmed with sadness and doubt. This, I could not deal with. *Cancer had beaten me before.* Now, here it was again, right in my face, consuming this man, a man I was sent to bring hope to. But how could I bring him the hope of healing when I had none myself?

Instead of sensing authority over this disease, I was cowering inside. In the place of faith I only had doubt. That doubt stood victorious over the confidence I had in almost every other dark situation we encountered in our work.

I told God that He had sent the wrong man. I was going to fail again.

An intense urgency came over me to convince Roberto to get saved because I knew he was just a few days from being dead. I did not want him to go to hell. At least I could pour all my soul into leading him to Jesus.

After all, the greatest miracle is when someone submits his life to Jesus and begins a relationship with Him. This is what drives me. We must win them or their destiny is eternal damnation. This is our command and our principal message, and the driving force behind all we do.

We are also commanded to bring healing to the afflicted, and that is what I had been trained to do. Over and over, we had seen Jesus enter the hearts of pagans and bring healing power with Him. Over 90 percent of the believers in our churches in Mexico have either been healed themselves, had someone they know healed, or had some other miraculous encounter with God.

I believe that healing is inseparable from redemption. Living and working with a people who are very spiritual and not so rational has taught me that I do not have to have everything figured out. And I do not fall apart spiritually if someone we pray for does not get healed. I examine myself, make sure I am living pleasing to God, and rest in the fact that God does what He knows is best. Then I aggressively approach the next problem with faith and confidence that Jesus is going to respond with the miraculous. And many times He does.

The only way our ministry advances at all is by an open show of the power of God. We witness extraordinary power because Jesus is alive.

This was my spiritual context when I sat, drowning in doubt, in the hut with this dying man.

The training that I'd received over the previous seven years pushed its way to the surface, and I was able to lead Roberto and his wife to Jesus. I told Roberto and his family that Jesus can do anything, and we gave him testimony after testimony of the power of God. I did that because the fact that Jesus heals is the Truth. I did that because that is what I believe about God, and Jesus, and the Gospel. But I also listened sadly to the words coming out of my mouth, because I was convinced that there was something wrong with *me*. I had confidence in Jesus. The problem was me.

But because of my training and raw obedience, I laid my hands of doubt on Roberto's tumor-swollen neck and asked God to heal him. I have laid hands on thousands of people. That fact helped me. At least I was saying the right thing, and doing the right thing, at the right time, and in the right place.

But I left that hut in tears, crying because all this man had to lay on were hand-cut boards. Crying because he was trapped by this killing disease. Crying because I was impotent in my faith and knew he was going to die. Crying because I felt that some other missionary would not be saddled with my limitation. Crying, too, because I felt I had failed my sister. Now I would fail Roberto.

I was also, somehow, determined. As I climbed up the side of that thick jungle canyon, my faith started to wrestle with my doubt. I decided to fast and pray, and call out to Jesus to respond in spite of my doubt, because that is what you do. You seek God. It's not about having flawless faith and it's certainly not about what we feel. It's about Jesus, and who He is.

———

I had planned a return visit with Roberto two days later. That was also something I'd been trained to do: keep praying until something happens, no matter how long it takes. I'm not sure what confused person came up with the idea that if you pray more than once for something that means that you don't have faith. That is not even scriptural![15]

By the time I got back to my house, I was resolved to plead Roberto's case with God. So I told Audrey and the kids. As I've mentioned, this work is our work—we do it together. So all of us, in our daily, morning prayer and worship, began praying for Roberto.

Prayer, worship, and the Word are the only true assets we have for connection with God. Without them we die.

"Pray, fast, and worship mostly and when you leave the house you will see Me work." That's what He said. That's what we did.

After two days Tino and I approached Roberto's hut, wondering if he was still alive. I called out a greeting to hail the house. A few moments later he appeared in his doorway from inside. Roberto smiled and invited us in. He seemed to be walking with purpose and strength. *Was he better?* Two days ago, he could barely sit up and talk with us.

---

[15] Luke 18:1-5

We entered his dark hut again and sat down. Roberto sat in the same blue plastic chair. I sat on the same eight-inch tall wooden stool. I looked at the same table full of idols and incense. I saw the same bushel of corn kernels. I heard the same sound of hands slapping in the kitchen—as his mother and wife made tortillas over a fire. I saw the same little girl swinging in her homemade crib hung by homemade hemp ropes from log poles. The roof was a mix of corrugated tarpaper and local clay roof tiles held on by their own weight. I saw the corners of the room coated with spider webs. I saw sunlight streaming through the open spaces between the hand-sawn boards of their walls, making pillars of light in the swirling smoke of their cooking fire. I watched the mound of corn masa diminish as hands slapped flat the tortillas that are a staple for millions in Mexico.

I rested my feet on the hard, uneven rock floor of this house. I saw the light blue sheet of plastic forming a "room" around the bed of the family patriarch. I saw the front door that had string for hinges and dragged the ground when it opened or shut. I saw the jungle through the open back door. Outside were large plastic garbage cans that held the water that was carried in a five-gallon bucket on the head of this man's wife, from thirty minutes away.

Along a wall I saw the back-carried stacks of firewood cut with machetes, and dried ears of corn hanging from rafters five feet from the floor. I saw the one shelf in the house, hanging also from the rafters, laden with the treasures of the indigenous people that populate these remote mountains: A family photograph vainly wrapped in plastic, fading with the infiltration of humidity laden air; two books; baptism certificates from the Catholic church; two straw hats used when working a cornfield; a file for sharpening machetes. These are poor people who have so little.

I saw also a man sitting in front of me, smiling, strong, moving as if he was not weak. *Could it be?* I wondered. I listened to forty-five minutes of small talk in a mixture of Nahuatl and Spanish, which is common with these Indians and their simple life.

I also saw something that changed my understanding of the way I think about faith, healing, and the power of God. I sat there with a growing sense of hope, faith, love, courage, victory, and pure joy. In my heart I moved from doubt to faith because, right in front of me sat Roberto, a man who should have been dead but who was alive.

Faith is not the absence of doubt. It is right action in the face of your doubt.

I *saw* the place on the side of his neck where I had placed my doubt-filled hands, my hands without power, the hands of a failure…and there was no tumor there.

Roberto was healed.

Faith is not the absence of doubt. It is right action in the face of your doubt.

9

Seeds

I had started off in the fight against cancer with my sister full of faith and confidence, but the progression of disappointing events had moved me from faith to doubt. When God healed Roberto of throat cancer, He moved me back from doubt to faith. This is yet another example of the ongoing, wonderful story of redemption, the reverse-order plan of God.

You may wonder how I could have a struggle like this when we had seen so much of God's power. How could I now be sweltering in doubt and defeat? Why? Because I'm no different than anyone else—our hearts are frail and our nature corrupted. We are human and fallen from glory.

Since we arrived at this new mission field in 2003, our new believers had prayed for six people who were raised from the dead. Jesus is indeed alive and uses us in our frailties. His love knows no bounds!

I believe Jesus came to work us back to Himself in the reverse order from God's original plan. Adam, in the Garden of Eden, had a perfect relationship with God, walking in undisturbed harmony with the Father every day. I don't think Adam had any faith or belief issues. He was created perfect, without fault and totally pleasing to God. Both God and Adam craved relationship with each other. Then Adam went from perfect to corrupt, from holy to fallen, from faith to doubt. So God unveiled a plan to work mankind from doubt to faith, from fallen to holy, from corrupt to perfect.

All of this had little to do with any person's ability to find relationship with God, and everything to do with God's ability to establish a relationship with an individual.

————

It is my joy and privilege to wrestle with how to communicate the mysteries of God to unbelievers. As I struggle through language and cultural barriers to make disciples, it is my responsibility to submit to God and respond to what He is doing, not what I think should be done. It is my responsibility to yield my mouth to the Holy Spirit so that as I teach the Bible, truth is delivered straight to the heart with clarity. As I began to disciple Roberto I wrestled to find the best way to explain faith to him.

I believe that's what the gifts and talents of God are for—to *respond* to the situations that develop from obedience—not to use our gifts to create situations. I want to follow Jesus, not my gifts. This pressure to speak God's words in a transforming way for the good of people is what prompts revelation knowledge to dawn in our own hearts. This struggle fosters dependence upon God, and dependence upon God opens His heart to *reveal*. As Jesus works, it draws you into a vacuum—a place void of all other power except the power of God. Responding to all of this while running after Jesus is why we have gifts and talents.

The collective teaching that I had heard all my life about faith and doubt did not fit with what had happened in my life in regard to my sister. Always before I was left with the unwinnable struggle to try to banish doubt, which is not possible. It is actually doubt that proves the existence of faith.

I watch so many people in Mexico work crop harvest cycles. These people have such an embedded capacity to understand many things that remain abstract and theoretical to modernized, urban people.

On my third visit to Roberto's I brought my family so that they could see the miracle they had prayed for. Audrey and the kids sat on small homemade stools and listened with joy. I sat in front of his idol table and responded to a question Roberto had. As I began to teach about faith, I looked over and saw his family's bushel bag full of corn kernels. *Seeds*. I looked from the seeds to the idols and back, and then it hit me—Jesus spoke to me, "Faith is like a seed." I got the *message!* God showed me a way to explain to this man, and others, the deep and complicated truth of how faith works in a way he could understand, in a way he could relate to. Indeed, I too, for the first time in my life, understood something profound about faith!

I flipped open my Bible to Mark 4:26-32 and began to read. Then I flipped to Matthew 17:14-20, followed by Romans 12:3. Sitting in that simple hut, hidden on the side of a forgotten canyon, the Spirit of God unlocked something to me so that I could explain faith to a man who lives in close harmony with the earth. These farmers live by planting seeds, then cultivating plants and finally harvesting. They are subsistence farmers. All of their cultivation is done by the use of their hands with simple tools: a machete, a hoe, and a stick with a steel point on the end. With these simple tools they work with seeds and the dirt to bring out of the ground the food that will sustain them. They have the capacity to understand the complex mystery of faith, because every year, via the crop cycle, they have a perfect example of faith seen in real life experience.

I looked at Roberto's idol table again. There were about twelve idols on it, each one with a specific identity, each having a unique purpose in this man's pagan beliefs. They place a bit of trust in each idol, some more than others, believing that the composite of their faith will increase their chances that God will respond with what they want, need, or desire.

So, I began to explain faith to this new believer using corn as the example because corn is their staple crop. From it the bread that sustains life is made. I asked Roberto for two kernels of corn from his bushel bag of seeds. I took out my pocketknife and cut one of the kernels into four pieces, held them out to him and asked, "What will happen if I go and plant these four pieces?"

"Nothing. Nothing will grow," he answered.

"Why?"

Divided faith cannot work because faith is a seed, and seeds only germinate if they are planted whole in good soil.

"Because you killed the seed when you cut it into pieces." I then showed him in the Bible that faith is like a seed, and that if we divide our faith, and try to "plant" it in different places, it cannot produce anything. Divided faith cannot work because faith is a seed, and seeds only germinate if they are planted whole in good soil. So we must put our whole faith only in God. Faith works like a seed.

Roberto smiled and his eyes lit up. Faith now made sense to him.

I have thought so many times in my life that if I had the faith, or gifts, or talents I saw in others then I could accomplish the things God was asking of me. All of the faith teaching that I'd ever heard or read about centered on banishing doubt or determining the amount of an individual's faith. But if it's the *amount* of faith that is our focus, then we easily sink under the ever-increasing weight of comparison. We will endlessly compare ourselves to each other, which is something we should never do. We should always compare ourselves to Jesus.

I am not saying that getting more faith is bad. I, too, want all of the faith I can get. But I'm convinced now that faith does not work based on an *amount*. It does however work by *percentage*. If it is God who works the impossible, then really how much faith is enough? And where does it specify an amount? Nowhere in Scripture can you find written how much faith it takes, as far as increasing amounts go. The only place where an amount is referred to is small, not big.[16] So no one can apply some type of measure to faith. Not even God has specified this.

However, what He has stated, over and over again, is that faith is quantified by percentage. That is why when Jesus likened faith to a mustard seed He was not talking about size but about potential in percentage. Whatever you have is enough; just make sure you put it all in Him—100 percent.

I told him that faith, like a seed, is like that also. If you want more faith then you have to plant 100 percent of the seed you have in good soil, and that good soil is Jesus.

All of the people there, the family members and those who had come with me, heard this explanation. They were listening and understanding!

When the Spanish conquered the Aztec empire, they conquered all of the slave-state nations, just as had the Aztecs before them. This perpetuated a long cycle of subservience for the indigenous residents of the nation. As a result, the flat, arable land was taken over by the conquerors, and the indigenous people were pushed into the mountains to find land for their crops. Consequently, some of their cornfields are on extreme mountain slopes as steep as seventy degrees! These farmers grow their corn on treacherous slopes where it would be

---

[16] Matthew 17:20

impossible to run a tractor. As they farm, they plant seeds. The seeds germinate, take root, grow, and produce a crop.

I continued with the agricultural example and I asked Roberto, "How many corn seeds are there on an ear of corn?"

"It depends on the size of the ear, but one like this," and he held up a dried ear, "has about 500 seeds on it."

"So if I plant one corn seed, then I am going to get lots of seeds on the ear of corn, from that one I planted?"

"Of course," he said, "there is always an abundance of seeds that come from the one seed you plant."

"What happens if you plant the corn seed in bad ground?" I asked.

"The seed would probably not grow."

One of my new and growing pastors was listening closely, and he got the message. Since that day he has prayed and seen many miracles and won many people to Jesus. He has seen the dead raised, not because he compared himself to great healing evangelists or to me, but because he planted the faith seed he had in the soil of Jesus.

I sat there listening to words flow out of my mouth that I did not have the wisdom to create. That day changed me. I had first come to that hut expecting the worst, and instead encountered something astounding. I came there dressed in the ashes of defeat. I left there wearing something beautiful—something touched by the glory of the Almighty.[17] In subsequent visits my family and I continued teaching Roberto, and others who were listening, about faith being like a seed.

Becoming the Message in living form is dependent upon Jesus opening your mind so that you can understand.[18] Diligent study of the

---

[17] Isaiah 61:3, Hebrews 4:12

[18] Luke 24:45

Scripture alone cannot give you that, but diligently seeking to *know* Jesus will.[19]

Praise filled my soul. Truth had dawned in me. The Truth is alive. The Truth is not merely correct information. The Truth is a Spirit.[20]

As I climbed out of that canyon, how very different were my thoughts than the first time I'd left that man's house. Heaviness had been replaced by power. Maybe God *was* going to use me to bring His presence to these people. Maybe it was not about my lack, but about Who I trusted in.

[19] John 5:39-40

[20] John 16:13

10

First Things First

After Armando was saved—the man who sold Audrey the armadillo purse—his brother-in-law, Sebastian, was born again as well. I had given him and his wife a ride and as they got in the truck I handed him a gospel tract. The tract piqued his curiosity and after we got to town, they sat and listened as I explained the plan of salvation. He accepted the message and prayed with me to accept Jesus.

Sebastian was concerned about the Bible that he had at his house. He wanted me to go to his house with him and verify that it was the right Bible. He knew that the Catholics have a Bible, and the Mormons have a Bible, and the Jehovah's Witnesses have a Bible, but he wanted to make sure that the Bible that he had was the same one that I read to him when he prayed to accept Jesus.

So I went with Sebastian to his house. As we were walking through his village, we passed by a neighbor's house. He called out to his neighbor, Tino, to come and hear what I had to say. We went inside Sebastian's house, and he called his family into the main room to listen to what I had to say. He grabbed his Bible and handed it to me and said, "Check it to see if this is the same Bible you have." So I checked, and it was. He said, "Tell them what you told me." So I began to explain, point by point the plan of salvation.

About that time, Tino came up to the door of Sebastian's house. He walked in and sat down in the empty chair beside me. He had been drinking moonshine, like countless other men in villages all over Mexico, and was a bit drunk.

Hope is a fleeting thing when you are draped with the choking sludge and manacles of oppression and poverty. The devil bends the search for hope and significance into despair for those who have no access to Jesus or elect not to accept the great hope that He is. He does this through the bottle of alcohol, or the needle of drugs, or through inflaming materialism fed by selfish corruption. This is why we are *sent* to *seek out* the lost. If I had not gone to Sebastian's house, I never would have met Tino. Salvation came next door to his house, and he stumbled through the fog of darkness into the glorious Light.

As I continued to explain the first steps of the Gospel, they were all attentive in the room, but Tino more so than all the rest. He wanted to see the Scripture with his own eyes, so I showed him in my Bible all of the Scriptures I was reading so he could see that it is written and that I was not speaking on my own.

As I finished, everyone in the room prayed to accept Jesus. Only one person there, however, really meant what he prayed. Tino really began his relationship with Jesus that day.

Shortly after that visit, the others there who prayed with me decided that they could not follow Jesus and opted to continue in their idolatry and witchcraft. The story of their lives from that point on is full of strife and despair and death. Tino's story is full of struggle, miracles, new hope, and life.

I visited Tino several times within the first three weeks after he prayed to receive Jesus. His wife was not at all interested in what I had to say, however. This is often the case, as many see us, and the Gospel, as threats to their traditions. Jesus is a threat to every idea that is contrary to Himself.[21]

---

[21] Luke 20:18, 1 Peter 2:8

One evening, as I sat in this new believer's house, his wife, Maria, came out to greet me and then sat down to listen. I could tell she was in pain, and then I noticed the golf-ball-sized bulge protruding from her lower jaw. I learned that Maria had been battling this severe tooth abscess for three weeks. Tino had taken her to the local clinic and gotten a prescription but the medicine had not helped. The pain and swelling had become unbearable.

While Maria had never come out and listened to what I was saying to her newly-saved husband, she had heard me talk because their house was very small. They had one room separated into two by a wooden wardrobe and a piece of material hung on a string. Consequently, she remembered what I'd said about Jesus being able to heal. Her pain now drove her to the Cross.

I asked Maria if she remembered what I had said about healing. She nodded her head. We preach that healing is inseparable from the Gospel message. I asked her if that is what she wanted. She nodded again. So I shared in detail with her the plan of salvation from the Scripture, and she accepted Jesus that night. Now she too was born again! Then I laid my hand on her head and simply asked Jesus to heal her tooth. The prayer lasted about fifteen seconds. I finished my coffee and left.

Five days later I was again at that house, and Maria and Tino related to me how Jesus had touched her the night she got saved. She had slept peacefully and awakened the next morning completely healed! That was the first miracle that happened in our new home. Maria has been faithful to Jesus ever since.

———

Rarely do I know what I am going to find when I leave my home and venture out with the purpose of winning souls.

On one occasion I set up a day of evangelism with a couple of our national workers, a visitor from America, and Kenny Carter, another missionary who was helping me in the work. I drove to the target community and parked my truck. We got out and began to visit people whom the native brothers knew. The first hour-long visit yielded a decision for Christ.

We continued to other houses. Most listened politely to what we had to say but were not willing to commit. That's normal; we talk to many and only a few respond. We continued in this manner for hours, first greeting, then explaining, then leaving to go to another house. Some people were very interested and curious to hear what we had to say. Others were filled with hatred and slammed the door in our face or threatened us.

To house after house we made our way, slowly and patiently, drinking a dozen cups of coffee as we did our best to win souls.

It came time for me to leave because I had a service scheduled in another village, in another part of the county that night. I felt that some of us should continue working house to house for the rest of the day, ending by walking back to our town when they were finished.

I left the visitor there with Kenny and the brother[22] who knew many people who lived in those communities. They continued to walk and witness of the good things God was doing amongst us. As they moved from house to house, they came to an especially small, poor house perched on the downhill slope of a mountain.

This indigenous house was very simple, just some bamboo and branch poles holding up corrugated tarpaper walls and roof. On the inside the ceiling was covered with cooking fire soot and spider webs. The floor was the clay ground from which they had dug their socket

---

[22] Christian national

from the hill, a place where they could cover their children and them-selves from the rain.

In response to their hailed greeting a woman appeared from inside and invited them in. As they entered the small ten-by-fifteen foot struc-ture, they saw the woman's husband lying on a bed of blankets laid on hand-sawn boards. He was extremely weak, not able to raise his head. He just rolled his head over and looked at the people as they entered.

This man, his name was Herman, had a bandanna tied over his mouth, which was a curious and rare thing to see. It came to light that he had been bedridden for four months, unable to work. His family was in trouble, as he was their sole provider. Our brothers recognized this as a real opportunity for the power of God.

The problems people have are usually our greatest evangelists, often driving people to the Cross out of their desperation for help. They began to explain the plan that God laid out for our salvation, and how the hope of healing is inseparably associated with the message of the Gospel of the Lord Jesus Christ.

The problems people have are usually our greatest evangelists, often driving people to the Cross out of their desperation for help.

Herman had tuberculosis. That's why he had his mouth covered with a bandanna, It hurt his lungs to inhale straight air, so they placed a barrier over his mouth to heat the air a bit to make it easier for him to breathe. Our team learned that Herman's mom, dad, and brother had all died with tuberculosis. Essentially, he was slowly dying, fading away behind a cheap cotton veil.

Jesus died to tear open every veil, removing every separation between God and us. He bore a terrible beating in order to purchase healing power for us!

Nearing death, Herman accepted the invitation to meet Jesus. After that every seven days one of our faithful brothers or myself went to his house to read him the Bible and pray for him.

We returned week after week, reasoning with his wife, Luz, a Jehovah's Witness, about her salvation, battling for her soul. She watched us return repeatedly and pray for her husband. Every visit pushed back a little more the death throes that were waiting to wrap this man in their final grip. Every week he got better and better.

This continued for four months. The power of God easily bent this disease over like a green sapling so that everybody around this man was convinced that the love of God has no rival.

His whole family is now born again. He is on fire for God. He's well. He is able to work. His smile is infectious. He testifies to all he meets of how God first saved, and then healed him.

Jesus can do anything.

————————

When we approach the sick and needy, we do not just pray for the sick and hope that they get the message of Jesus. Healing is a part of redemption, and therefore we preach redemption first and foremost.[23] Normally, unless I am directly led by the Holy Spirit, I do not pray for healing until a person prays to receive Christ. Healing was purchased at the Cross. I never want to step on the blood of Jesus by allowing a healing to supplant salvation in a person's mind. Many people want immediate physical relief but don't want to make Jesus their Lord. The Bible lays out the order: Preach, then heal.

In the Mexican culture there are many types of people praying for the sick. In fact, there is a complete economy surrounding prayer for

---

[23] Isaiah 53:3-5, Matthew 10:7-8

the sick and afflicted. We don't charge fees to pray for people, but all the others do.[24] The Catholic priests charge, witch doctors charge, and spiritist healers charge. Even the Catholic reciters, who will come to your house and find specific prayers out of the Catholic book of prayers and pray for various situations, demand payment for their useless services. All of these types of people claim to have the answer, but none of them do.

We could spend all our days going from house to house praying for people and be swamped with needs, and they would never have a reason to believe because there would be no distinction between what we do and what all these other people do in the name of a "god."

We must make the message of Jesus clear. When Jesus sent His disciples out He told them to preach first, then heal the sick.[25] If the Lord wants to change the order of that, it's His business. In all the years I have been preaching the Gospel, He has rarely told me to pray for the sick before preaching or sharing the Good News.

We have to preach first, or we would never have time to preach at all because of the needs all around us. In every home I've ever visited there's a problem the people need Jesus to fix. Sickness, witchcraft, economic or social problems saturate every household. Their plight is usually desperate, and only Jesus can help them emerge from the darkness that consumes them. It is relationship with Jesus that will bring them out, not only a miracle. The wondrous, visible power of God is designed to help facilitate the reality of relationship with Him.

Nothing can compare with serving and knowing a living Savior.

Nothing.

---

[24] Matthew 10:8

[25] Matthew 10:7-8

11

God's Mysterious Ways

In 1999, our oldest daughter, Hannah, fell sick with an ongoing fever that briefly spiked to 106 degrees. She remained sick for three weeks with an intermittent high fever and was so weak that we feared for her life.

She struggled for over a year. At times she would feel better for a few days and begin to play, but then she would relapse and crawl back into bed in her weakness. She had no strength and spent much of her time in pain in bed. She would crawl from her bedroom across the hall to the living room, where we would meet for family prayer and worship. This was never diagnosed, but seemed like Chronic Fatigue Syndrome. Later, when we got to the States, Hannah's blood work showed she had had mononucleosis at some point. It seems it was that plus more, but we will never know for sure the name of the problem we faced.

We felt helpless.

We were into our second year in Mexico, and this was the first test of this magnitude we'd faced. I was seeing so many miracles in our work in villages, yet here was my daughter suffering and so weak she had to drag herself across the floor. When we traveled as a family to work in villages, Audrey had to put Hannah on her back and carry her to the outhouse. All I knew was to keep moving forward in ministry and all of life.

Some people wonder how we could stay when our children were suffering. The real question is how could we leave if Jesus didn't say to. Circumstances aren't the voice of God. He said go. We went. He did not say leave. We stayed.

———

Shortly after the 2001 terrorist attacks on the World Trade Center, Pentagon, and the plane crash in Pennsylvania, our missionary team was staying all together for security reasons at the ministry headquarters ranch in central Mexico. Hannah had finally begun showing some improvement, and she and several other missionary children were playing outside on a tire swing. Hannah was swinging on that tire swing when the rope broke and she fell hard to the ground with her feet tucked underneath. The tire smashed into her left foot. We thought she might have fractured it, but the x-ray of the foot was not of very good quality and somewhat vague.

Weeks went by and the pain in Hannah's foot got worse. We came out of Mexico to the United States and had her foot checked by a doctor in south Texas. He thought it was possible that she had a fracture and suggested an MRI. We didn't have the money for that, so he put her foot in a cast to protect it.

Days went by and still the pain intensified. Something was not right, so Audrey took her to another doctor. He took the cast off and saw a smaller than normal, violet-colored, hypersensitive little foot. Touching her toe caused immense pain. He x-rayed her foot again and positioning her foot caused her even more pain. The doctor told Audrey that her bones looked like an 80-year-old woman with osteoporosis. He'd never seen a patient with this but remembered from medical school about Reflex Sympathetic Dystrophy (RSD), a nervous system injury. She had all the signs and symptoms.

We consulted with Audrey's dad, a pediatrician, who was living at the time in Atlanta, Georgia. He researched RSD and informed us that if she in fact had it, then her condition was indeed very rare and serious. In his thirty-five years of working with children he had never seen a case. He worked it out so that we could take her to a specialist in San Antonio, Texas, who had experience with this rare condition. That doctor confirmed that she did indeed have RSD.

RSD is an injury to the nervous system. Essentially, the pain signal that had switched on when the tire swing fell on Hannah's foot never shut off and grew in intensity. The specialist in San Antonio warned Audrey and me that we would need to begin the slow and painful process of resetting Hannah's nervous system, and that we had to start immediately.

If RSD progresses more than three months, for most people it essentially becomes irreversible, and in some cases, the affected limb has to be amputated. Hannah had been injured for over two months, and her pain was so bad that even the vibrations of musical sound waves coming from a radio or instrument would cause her to cry. Another person walking across a plywood floor would cause her to wince in pain because of the movement in the floor. The weight of a sheet touching the end of her toe at night was more than she could bear.

Audrey and I steeled ourselves to begin the physical therapy that the doctor had prescribed. We knew this was going to be hard, but we had no idea just how difficult.

We returned to Mexico a couple of days later. Basically, in order to reset Hannah's nervous system, we had to stimulate her foot. This was not something that she wanted because it meant that we had to hurt her foot on purpose. It was terrible. Imagine inflicting pain on your child day after day.

I only know that there is no fault in God. He is good, no matter what circumstances seem to say.

Of course, during all of this we continued to cry out in faith for God to heal our little girl. I did not understand why God would not heal Hannah when I was seeing so much healing power in the work we were doing in villages! I didn't have an answer then and I don't now. I only know that there is no fault in God. He is good, no matter what circumstances seem to say. We were living clean before Him, praying for the sick and afflicted and seeing dramatic things happen. Miraculous things! So all we knew to do was not quit and to keep moving forward.

It was puzzling and hard. In case you haven't noticed, God is not always easy to figure out. However, it does not matter what I perceive or understand. He is God and I have settled that issue. I allow nothing to cast a shadow on my core decisions about Him. He is God, His Word is infallible the way it is written, and I trust Him no matter what happens to me or anybody else.

We began giving Hannah her therapy every day. Audrey is the one who had to carry out most of her physical therapy. This would go on all day, every day for almost a year. I would return from villages to help in the evenings. Audrey would almost collapse in my arms and cry in private, because of the pain Hannah was in.

The progress was slow and painful. We had to force Hannah to soak her foot in hot water and then ice cold water. We had to massage her foot and she was very brave. We had to make her stand on the injured foot. We put a scale under her foot to verify she was putting enough weight on it. As she made progress we had to continually push into the pain threshold so the pain signal could "learn" where the pain boundaries were and diminish.

The process was terribly slow. As Hannah gained the ability to support her weight on her foot for more than a few seconds, we began to lead her into taking steps. At first it took her thirty minutes to take ten steps, all the while crying and begging us to stop. But she made progress.

The only thing that kept us at it for the year that it took to reset her nervous system was the knowledge that if we did not push her into her pain, she could possibly live with pain in her foot for the rest of her life.

This was the most difficult thing we ever had to do as parents, to intentionally have Hannah do things that caused her such pain. I cannot describe the joy we all felt the first time after her injury that we saw Hannah run!

Then Jesus really came and helped Hannah. In the summer of 2004 Hannah attended the three-day Desperation student conference held at New Life Church in Colorado Springs, Colorado. She had regained the full use of her foot and could walk, run, and jump, but she was still living with pain, especially when she jumped.

Hannah was in one of the main worship sessions at the conference when she decided to dance while worshiping Jesus. She made this decision even though she knew she was going to pay for it with more pain. As she began to jump and shout and worship with all of her heart, Jesus touched her! The pain—finally, after almost three years—fled her foot. She knew something had happened. She was free! She had worshipped her pain away never to return.

I cannot begin to explain God's ways or His timing. The Bible says in Psalm 34:19 that many are the afflictions of the righteous, but the Lord delivers him from them all. Sometimes, like the children of Israel in Judges 20, at God's direction, we go to war and get sent into battle and we lose that battle. And we run to God in anguish, and He sends

> If we stay the course and keep running and fighting against the same battle that defeated us, then we finally see a great victory.

us back into battle, only to lose again. We run back to God, and He again sends us into battle, this time with the promise of victory. If we stay the course and keep running and fighting against the same battle that defeated us, then we finally see a great victory. I'm always thankful when Jesus shows up and great things happen!

_____

Some years later, in the summer of 2009, Hannah and I went on a three-week backpacking expedition in Alaska. There I watched her carry over half her body weight on her back, bushwhacking day after day through the wilderness. I had not forgotten that she could have lost her leg. Thanksgiving flooded my soul that she could now walk with such confidence, pain free.

We must never quit when difficult things seize our lives.[26] We must keep moving. If we can't run, we walk. If we can't walk, we crawl. If we can't crawl, we lean forward. If we can't lean forward we think forward. We serve a mysterious God. It is our part to bow humbly and learn to accept His majesty and inscrutable, but awesome, ways. May our perseverance through pain and suffering bring Him glory!

[26] Psalm 24

12

Thanksgiving in Mexico

In November of 2003 a lady named Juana had heard that a "Gringo witch doctor" (that is what some of the people think I am), who could heal her of her diabetes, was coming to a village, a three-hour walk from her house.

The day of that meeting Juana came in a bit late after her long trek. She told me she had diabetes, she was having trouble controlling her blood sugar, and the disease was getting steadily worse.

I began to share the Gospel, telling Juana that Jesus could heal her, but that she needed to give her life to Him and be born again. She prayed that night to receive Jesus, and after I had prayed for her to be healed she invited me to her house. I immediately said yes! This meant an invitation into another new village—another opportunity for the living Lord Jesus to be more than a name on the pages of Scripture and who could begin to transform hell-bound souls!

I set up an appointment with Juana and the next week headed for her village. A couple of our new converts went along; one of them was Tino, whose cousin, Roberto, had been healed of throat cancer.

When we arrived at Juana's house she received us graciously and shared that she was feeling much better and had seen a doctor who had told her that she did not have diabetes anymore! He had asked her how that could be? He wanted to know if she had found a plant in the jungle that had cured her.

Juana answered, "No, I did not find a plant in the jungle. A man prayed for me in the name of Jesus, and the next day I felt like I was not sick anymore." Jesus had healed Juana's diabetes the day she got saved.

My family and I had a six-week trip to the United States scheduled in the next few days, so I left the initial follow-up visits in the hands of our new national believers. These national brothers, led by Tino, continued to visit Juana's house every week while we were gone to the United States. They taught the Bible and attempted to win her husband and children to Jesus.

She knew every sick person in her village, and was so excited about being healed that she wanted us to meet Paula, the sickest person in the area.

Juana was the health auxiliary for her village, which meant that she was a type of lay nurse—someone who has a bit of training and works for the local clinic dispensing vitamins, medicine, and medical supplies that a doctor would have prescribed on one of his infrequent visits to the local clinic. She knew every sick person in her village, and was so excited about being healed that she wanted us to meet Paula, the sickest person in the area.

When Tino and Pepe, another of our new believers, arrived for the third visit to Juana's house, she told them about Paula and asked if they would pray for her. They said yes and walked down the road and across a field to Paula's house where they found her suffering terribly with a viral skin infection known in tropical areas as "jungle rot." It is kind of like a slow growing gangrene. Juana had told Paula about being healed of diabetes and was confident that she could be healed as well.

When they were invited into the house, Paula unwrapped the bandage on her leg. Everybody saw that she had a huge open ulcer with extreme muscle, tendon, and bone invasion on her lower leg. The open ulcer on the front and side of her leg was about four inches wide and extended from just below her knee down past her ankle and onto her foot. The sore was so severe that her tibia could be seen in several places. The skin around the rest of the outside of her calf was black, tight, and hard. Paula had suffered with this condition for over twenty years, with the ulcer slowly deepening, opening more and more of her leg.

Tino and Pepe explained the Gospel to this afflicted lady, and Paula prayed with them and got saved. Then, in the name of Jesus, they prayed for her leg problem that had slowly worsened for two decades in spite of regular doctor visits. Then they set up another visit with her for a week later and left.

Tino and Pepe continued to visit Paula every time they visited Juana. Each visit in both places they would encourage the new believers present, try to win other family members to Jesus who had not been born again, and pray for needs—each time praying for Paula's leg. These inexperienced but learning pastors were gripped with compassion. They had already seen God heal cancer, diabetes, and a tooth abscess. They had read in the Bible how Jesus healed many, and that "all things were possible" with Him, so they simply did what I had been teaching them.

The brothers returned three times in two weeks. Each time they returned they found that the condition of Paula's leg was markedly improved. It was healing rapidly! The men were very encouraged and shared more of the Word of God with her and continued to pray for her leg. Beginning with the second visit to Juana's house, they walked through this process for five weeks in a row, each week setting up a date for a return visit.

That is what we do. We go and keep going. This is how Jesus builds His Church. By this time, the brothers knew that my family and I were due back from our trip to the United States, so they set up a visit for us to accompany them after we returned.

A week later Audrey, our son, David, and I went with these ambassadors of the Kingdom of God to find that God had closed up an unhealing, debilitating open wound in five weeks of praying! There was only a spot about the size of a quarter on Paula's ankle. The skin around her calf was restored, supple, and no longer black!

What an awesome, powerful, and living God we serve! He had created that woman's leg in the first place, and He knows how to fix anything He made!

In later visits we observed that even the small spot on her ankle disappeared within a few months.

As it turned out, Paula lived and worked on the cattle ranch of a wealthy man from our town. He and his brothers found out that a "gringo" was visiting one of their employees, and they instructed the head cowboy to forbid us entry! Give me a break! That irritated me! Usually, the wealthy in Mexico don't really care for the people they employ in this capacity. So often they only think about themselves. I also knew that it was the enemy working to shut down an opportunity for the Gospel. But we could not go back.

So for months after that we prayed and prayed that God would open the door for us to return to that ranch to teach the Word of life to this newly healed convert. Every time we drove past there, we asked God to smite the heart of the owner so that Paula and the other workers could hear the Word of God.

———

That fall Audrey began giving English lessons to a few children in our town. Ever the soulwinner, Audrey was thinking about how she might make a clear presentation of the Gospel to the families of her students. We were still new in this place, and were also using these classes to help establish our credibility in the community, to help people get to know who we were.

Audrey got the idea to host the students' families for a Thanksgiving dinner as an American cultural experience and use that time as an opportunity to share the Gospel message with both her students and their family members. So we got busy and planned a Thanksgiving dinner complete with turkey, dressing, broccoli salad, sweet potato casserole (with the local purple sweet potatoes), pecan pie, and more.

> Everyone filled their plates with the strange food and sat around our tables. Before we ate I said a prayer of thanks to the Lord.

Thanksgiving Day arrived and about twenty-five people came to our house from the community. Everyone filled their plates with the strange food and sat around our tables. Before we ate I said a prayer of thanks to the Lord. That I would pray like this was foreign to them, and they were respectfully surprised when I did. In their world only Catholic priests or reciters said prayers in public.

We began to eat our meal amid some questions about the reason for this American holiday dedicated to thanking God. I was sitting next to an obviously wealthy landowner and rancher named Mario. He also owned a store in our town.

Between bites of turkey he asked me, "What do you do? We see you often coming and going in your truck, your Jeep, or on your motorcycle."

"I preach the Gospel," I answered.

"The Gospel, what is that?"

That question thrilled me! We had been praying for open doors into these people's hearts. Audrey had been praying for them by name for months. To have someone ask about the Gospel and show some interest is a miracle that only God can work. We are always ready to talk about the Gospel.[27]

This was the very reason we had decided to have this cultural experience for the parents of Audrey's English students, to share with them the Good News. We had begun to see God at work in this community. People were born again, miraculous healings had occurred that included a woman's severe tooth abscess, Juana healed of diabetes, Roberto at the brink of death healed of throat cancer, and of course Paula with the jungle rot. I took out my Bible and began to explain to the rancher exactly what we did, weaving in the Scriptures about salvation.

The others at the table, some of them also from prominent families in our town, listened as I gave the clearest description of the message that I could. These people were not the indigenous people we meet with in the mountains. These folks were the upper-class people of political and economic influence who owned businesses, held positions in the community, and had very strong influence in our town and county. This was a rare opportunity to share Jesus with them. Although our main ministry focus was on the indigenous tribes, our commission was to win anyone who would listen about and respond to Jesus.

So there I sat at my table on Thanksgiving Day, sharing the testimony of those healed and delivered, not knowing that at my elbow was the wealthy owner of the ranch where Paula was healed. Without realizing whom I was talking to I shared the testimony of the lady who'd been healed of jungle rot. Mario shot a look at his wife and then back at me and asked, "Where was that ranch? What was the name of the place?"

---

[27] 2 Timothy 4:2

I told him the name and he said, "I think that is my ranch!"

I explained more of the situation and he said that it was definitely his place and that he had paid for the lady's doctor's visits for twenty years. Mario looked at his wife and said, "You know, Paula has not asked to go to the doctor in months."

"It's because the Lord has healed her," I said.

"I am going to ask her what has happened," he said pensively.

We continued our conversation, and Mario became even more interested in what I was telling him and asked me questions for three hours! At the end of the evening, an hour and a half after all the other guests had left, he and his wife invited our family to go to his house for a meal.

Mario went to his ranch and found out that indeed Paula had been healed.

We accepted his invitation to dinner, knowing that Jesus was working on Mario's heart. We had been praying for him by name as a parent of Audrey's student, as well as when we passed his ranch, not knowing that it was the same man. God is always at work. His will is that all men might be saved!

About three weeks later we found ourselves sitting in Mario's dining room with an abundance of food arranged on a beautiful table. We felt a bit out of place since this was the first time we were in the home of someone in the upper class. I sat down with my plate full of food, and the man said to me, "Would you please pray that beautiful prayer that you prayed when we were at your house?"

I told him it would be my honor to pray, but I could not pray that exact prayer because when we pray, it comes from our heart and we don't use memorized prayers. This was something he had never heard, because for him all prayers were written down in a book, memorized, and selected for appropriate occasions. Mario knew those prayers seemed dead. For the first time in that house, I think, communication with the Son of God happened.

After praying I began to explain to Mario and his wife and two young sons that we do not have religion but instead a personal relationship with a living God. Again, for over three hours we testified and witnessed to the greatness of God. We reasoned with this man and his family with the Scriptures.

I could see spiritual hunger building in him. He kept asking questions about what I do. At the end of the night, I said to him, "If you are so interested in what I do, then why don't you go with me sometime?"

"I would love to," Mario answered.

1 3

The Miracle of Chicken and Rice

I became a bit of a friendly nuisance to Mario. In addition to his ranch, he and his wife, Daniela, had a store in town. For the next couple of weeks when I passed their store I would stop and invite him to go to service with me. Each time I asked, he politely evaded the opportunity.

Dani told him that he was embarrassing her by not accepting the invitation to go with me. Finally, he told her he would go, thinking that would get him off the hook with me. He would go see "what the crazy gringo was doing."

A couple of days later I stopped and again asked Mario if he wanted to come along, and he surprised me by saying yes and climbed into my truck.

I wondered what God was up to. A man like Mario is difficult to reach because members of his social class live an aristocratic lifestyle. Normally, it doesn't work well in Mexican society to try to mix people from this aristocratic class with indigenous people.

I did not know this rancher's background too well and only later would find out that he was not as aristocratic as some. I was excited and nervous at the same time and wondered if I was creating cultural tensions by bringing Mario to a village. Normally, people like him only go to villages if they have business there, or if they are involved in politics and are purchasing votes from the poor. The political environment in Mexico, like in many countries, is often full of wickedness and deceit, and I could not afford to be associated with this in the minds of the people. The county was full of rumors about what it was we were doing, and to have this man in my truck would only contribute to more wagging tongues.

We arrived at our destination and went into Tino's new one-room concrete block house where I had scheduled to have a service that night. There were only four people there besides Mario and me. We began the service with reading a Psalm and singing some simple songs that are kind of like "folk music" worship. The house was simple. The man leading worship was playing an out of tune guitar and singing off key. There was zero entertainment value or cultural relevance present, especially not any relevance to Mario's culture. There was just a handful of people there doing their best to worship and respond to God. I was clapping and singing and jumping during worship. Mario later related to me that he looked at me and thought, *These people are crazy. Look at this gringo. He is out of his mind!*

However, the Spirit of the Living God began to touch Mario. Before long he too began to clap, overcome by something that he had never felt. He was having an encounter with the Spirit of God, and he had never even conceived that there was such a thing. He had prayed all his life and never had any indication that there was any true validity to God. Mario even had made a pilgrimage every year, riding his horse from our town for seven days all the way to Mexico City to the temple of the Virgin of Guadalupe. But he never had encountered anything beyond his own flesh-filled experience. He also had carried a wooden cross around and around the cathedral in town, purposefully bruising and cutting his shoulder in order to get his place in Heaven assured.

Now Mario found himself in a humble indigenous house, clapping and moving to the worship music with tears running down his face. He stood in wonder, as such an encounter was in conflict with his pragmatics and his religion. Indeed, the whole religious experience of his life was dismantled and shown for a cheap imitation, unable to even cast a shadow's reflection of the truth.

The place we were in stood at extreme opposites to everything he knew or associated with God. The Catholics build extravagant cathedrals. Their idols are all vested in fine and expensive garments, many crowned with glorious adornments. The priests wear specially set apart robes and their world leader is held up as an earthly king. But here he was in a bare house, with zero comforts, listening to music that at best was a screech to his ears. And yet he was experiencing a wondrous encounter, something so majestic and astonishing that it crashed through his pride and arrogance—opening his blind eyes and deaf ears. The finger of the living God touched him, and for the first time in his life he felt the Holy Spirit! After serving dead religion all his life, thinking that he was serving God, the Spirit of God announced Himself to this man!

A humble indigenous man at the service, a man many social tiers beneath the rancher, asked Mario if he wanted to be born again. Because of his encounter with something real, something powerful, something eternal, Mario said yes, even though he had no idea what that meant for his future. He just responded to the call of his Creator, his God, his Savior.

He said yes even though it would turn those of his own family into enemies. He said yes because Jesus is no respecter of persons. He said yes, not because I had convinced him that the Bible is true and that he should believe because of the rightness of what I teach. No, Mario gave his heart to Jesus because he had an encounter with something real, something beyond himself, something devastating to his carnal nature.

After he got saved, Mario had many misconceptions, including a belief that Jesus would bless his life with all material abundance. He thought that because he valued material wealth, Jesus would make his life better by making him richer. His views about life were based on a temporal perspective. Therefore, since life meant money, women, houses, and trucks, then surely his surrender to Jesus would increase all of those things.

For sure, knowing God does bring abundance, but abundance of life in its truest sense. Jesus blesses the things that are eternal and that reflect the nature of God to those around us. This brother needed an adjustment of values, one that started shortly after he gave his heart to Jesus.

Mario was born again in early December of 2004, and soon after that his wife, Dani, and two sons were saved as well. The night that Dani gave her life to the Lord she cried huge tears as she wrestled with whether or not she could give her heart to Jesus. She wanted to follow her husband, but she was unsure. She said something we don't want to ever forget, "I know *about* Jesus, but I *love* the Virgin of Guadalupe." She was afraid that if she gave her life to Jesus she would have a big hole in her heart that the "Guadalupana" had always filled. All of the prayers and adoration of her life had been directed to the Virgin of Guadalupe. They even had a large ornate idol of her in their living room.

I told her that Jesus is patient. He would fill her heart so full that there would be no room for anyone else. She decided to give Jesus a chance and to stand with the decision her husband had made. She gave her life into God's hands. That night we also prayed for her leg. She suffered from deep vein thrombosis, a serious problem. She had been hospitalized and bedridden for weeks the year before and now was doing a lot better, but the doctors told her that she would have to live with a perpetually swollen and painful ankle. She wore an elastic band around her ankle to help with the swelling. Audrey squatted down and held her ankle and prayed for healing. Dani awoke the next morning without any swelling or pain! Jesus had healed her, and she remains healed to this day.

That was the first of many miracles this family has experienced. Jesus immediately began to prove Himself to these wealthy people who had few material needs.

In January of 2005 my family and I left to go to the United States to visit our supporters and broaden our support base.[28] I asked Mario if he would host a gospel campaign, a large meeting, at his house, and that another missionary was going to come and preach while we were gone. Mario had a huge patio behind his home that would be perfect for such an event. He gladly agreed but asked me what a campaign was. I explained that we were going to invite people to come together and worship God and listen to the Word of God preached.

Mario was happy to offer his house and asked if he needed to serve food. I told him that whatever he had in his heart to do was great, so he wanted to know how many people might come. I told him that I expected forty to fifty.

Mario and Dani decided to prepare chicken mole with rice. He bought eight chickens and two kilos of rice, enough to feed about eighty people. On the day of the campaign, people began to come. And come. And come. As more and more people came through his gate, Mario became more and more nervous, because in Mexican culture if you cannot feed everyone, it is a great embarrassment to the host and offense to the guests. The rancher had set up tables and had food for

---

[28] Itineration, Deputation

around eighty people, but the crowd swelled to over two hundred and fifty! Where did all these people come from?

Dani told those who were helping with the food that they were not going to be able to eat; there wasn't nearly enough food. Mario and his helpers began to give plates of food to the people seated at the tables. He was praying that somehow the food would last at least one serving. In the activity of serving two hundred and fifty people, he lost track of how many plates were distributed.

Mario was relieved to discover that all of the people had been served a full plate! He also noticed that his wife had gone ahead and served all the workers as well. He thought that Dani had discreetly ordered more chicken and rice from one of the small restaurants near their house.

"Did you order more food?" he asked her.

"No. I have no idea how, but it is okay, there is enough food," she said. And it now appeared that the amount of food left in the pots was the same as when they had served the first plate.

Mario went around to each table, as any good host always does, and asked everyone if they wanted more food, praying the whole time that no one would ask for more. To his terror, everybody wanted seconds! He hurried to the kitchen and asked if the food would last, and Dani said, "Let's just serve plates until it is all gone." So they kept up a steady flow until everybody had been served a second time, including all the workers.

That amounted to over five hundred plates of food from eight chickens, two kilos of rice, and tortillas—originally enough food to serve at most eighty people!

Jesus had multiplied the food! *He is the same yesterday, today, and forever!*[29]

---

[29] Matthew 14:15-21, Hebrews 13:8

I am always amazed at God's ability to demonstrate His love to us. Sometimes we think that God is only working on the big Heaven and hell issues of life, but God is present in the smallest minutia of our lives too, and He lacks no resources.

————

As is often the case with wealthy men of his social class who live in the rural, ranch-culture municipios (counties), Mario owned many horses, which were another source of pride and vanity for him. His favorite horse was sick and was being kept in the stock stalls at the end of his home's extended, roofed patio.

> Sometimes we think that God is only working on the big Heaven and hell issues of life, but God is present in the smallest minutia of our lives too, and He lacks no resources.

All the people who had come to the campaign were gathered under the patio roof and near the livestock stalls. This man's favorite horse had a serious condition, which the local veterinarian was attempting to treat. His spine was severely arched in an upward arc, such that the feet were drawn grossly together, causing the animal to stand on the front edges of its hooves.

We had invited a music group from a church in a neighboring municipio to come and lead praise and worship for the service. After everybody had eaten their two plates of food and the tables were cleared, the announcement was given that the service was going to start. Everyone reassembled at a prepared spot near the sick horse's stall.

The service began with a welcome by Mario, and an introduction of the worship team. Then the music started. Not long after the first song, the rancher heard a commotion from the horse stall. He looked back to see his sick and lame horse jumping and kicking and neighing along with the music. The animal was running back and forth in his stall, seeming to revel and frolic as if he were worshiping God!

Before the music had started, the horse could only stand and barely walk in one direction, much less kick and buckjump in rhythm with the music. His spine had resumed its normal and beautiful saddle-ready curvature! As long as the music played, that horse worshiped God. God *healed* that horse! Mario had planned soon to put the horse out of his misery because he only had worsened for weeks. Now, the horse was totally restored.

God had healed a rich man's horse, not because it was a beast of burden, a necessity that was desperately required for the livelihood of a poor family. Mario had many horses, but God healed that favorite horse just to tell the rancher that He loved him.

———

One last note about the food miracle: the campaign was held on a Saturday when 500 plates of food were served. Sunday, twelve people at Mario's house ate from the same food, and again on Monday, Tuesday, and Wednesday. On Thursday, Mario was entertaining a friend in his kitchen for breakfast, when Dani came in and said, "Let's call all the workers in here and give them five or six pieces of chicken each. I have had it up to here with chicken!"

All this from enough chicken and rice to feed just eighty people. Amazing.

14

Obedience

As I considered what seemed the almost impossible task of seeing the Gospel established in a place where it had not taken root before, the Lord spoke to me about obedience. Our commission from Jesus is to make disciples,[30] and since disciples are made and not born, that meant we needed to work for the establishment of local churches.

Evangelization is only the beginning of the process. In fact, it is the easiest part of the process. Our commission as believers is to teach everybody we lead to Jesus to obey His words. Obedience is both a daily and lifelong task. Everybody Jesus called He asked to *follow* Him. This is impossible without obedience.

In American Christianity we spend so much time, money, and effort teaching Christ followers *what* to obey that we have minimal resources left with which to train them *to* obey. We focus our energy on the sharing of information, which we think completes the "make disciples" part of the Great Commission. Of course, this information is vitally important, but after sharing the content, then comes training, much in the same way that we train our children.

---

[30] Matthew 28:16-20

The foundation of discipleship is *character.*

The development of character takes time. The church falls sadly short in the building of character because the training takes a long-term, personal interaction directly with those we disciple. We struggle because there is no "model" to easily duplicate. We get good at avoiding substantive lifelong relationships because it is disruptive to our personal privacy or the privacy of our families; so God sits by and watches us move forward without Him.

The vast majority of full-time church workers focus almost exclusively upon the execution of church services and leave relational discipleship to happenstance. But, disciples are made on purpose, and this is impossible without intrusive, privacy-disrupting relationship with others. That is what Jesus did. He broadcast His message to thousands, regularly taught His many followers, and lived 24/7 with His closest disciples. Likewise, we should preach to masses, teach many, and disciple a few.

The church makes disciples all right, but what are we discipling them to? We have figured out how to attract and hold crowds, and by doing so, have taught our disciples to expect certain services from the church or they won't attend.

We praise the brilliance of a church leader who can install systems and programs that rival the best found in corporate America, but often these operational structures become a substitute for the one-on-one personal discipleship of an individual. The focus is on the church service and programs instead of teaching believers to engage with each other. Christian families revolve around themselves rather than around their called ambassadorship. So many Christians focus first upon themselves rather than Jesus first, then others.

We reflect the values of society rather than transform them. It almost seems that we believe that our highest purpose is to call people to corporate morality and good citizenship rather than calling them to obedience to Jesus Christ. We do this and call it making disciples.

Jesus made us all responsible to make disciples. Yet, because of our distraction and preoccupation with the tangible things of this world and the many cares of this life, we have created a vast army of schooled men and women who are full of information but void of power. We believe that if people know *what* to obey, it will logically follow that they *will* obey.

The state of the modern church, collectively, is dangerously close to the same condition as that of the expert in religious law whose critical attitude toward Jesus was to test Him with his own knowledge and understanding of the Scripture:

> One day an expert in religious law stood up to test Jesus by asking him this question: "Teacher, what should I do to inherit eternal life?"
>
> Jesus replied, "What does the law of Moses say? How do you read it?"
>
> The man answered, "You must love the LORD your God with all your heart, all your soul, all your strength, and all your mind. And, love your neighbor as yourself."
>
> "Right!" Jesus told him. "Do this and you will live!" (Luke 10:25-28 NLT).

Jesus asked this man if he knew the Scriptures. He also asked how he understood the Scriptures. The man got both answers right, but knowing and understanding is not enough. This man knew *and* understood the Truth. His problem was not a problem of ignorance, but of execution. Jesus wants us to know what to do, and do what we know.

God's instructions are not so complicated that they require endless research and innovative programs. He gave simple instructions. Go.

Preach. Baptize. Make disciples. Teach them to obey My words. Do not charge for it. Do it until you die.

> The problem for most of us is not that we don't know what to do. It's about actually doing what we know, because the Kingdom of God is not about words but about power.

I once had a conversation with a young man who was wrestling with whether he should give up his life in order to serve Jesus outside his home culture. He was concerned that he might not have enough Biblical knowledge to advance the Gospel in a foreign country. He had been saved for years, so I asked him if he was attentive when he went to church. He said he had been. I then assured him that he had more than enough Bible knowledge to begin to advance the Gospel anywhere in the world.

The problem for most of us is not that we don't know what to do. It's about actually doing what we know, because the Kingdom of God is not about words but about power.[31]

When missionaries leave the mission field the problem is rarely, if ever, a lack of Bible knowledge. In fact, the number one problem that most missionaries face is that they cannot get along with their coworkers—other missionaries. Most of their interpersonal conflicts stem from personal character problems that cause obedience issues.

The Bible is full of instruction on getting along, but we must apply it. Ephesians 4:2-3 says, "Be completely humble and gentle; be patient,

---

[31] 1 Corinthians 4:20

bearing with one another in love. Make every effort to keep the unity of the Spirit through the bond of peace." Jesus prayed that there would be unity among us so that the world would see and know Him for who He really is.[32] We are commanded to serve one another humbly in love.[33] We are commanded to not be selfish, but with humility to consider others better than ourselves.[34] This is not easy. It's a daily choice to not be selfish.

The same lack of application exists in marriages. We are saturated with anointed marriage seminars and ministries, but too many Christians are not much better at marriage than those who are without Jesus. The divorce rate inside the church is horribly high. The problem is not one of information, but of transformation.

———————

I have two streams of intensity flowing inside of me that cause me to persuade people. The first is an urgency to let people know of this coming day of accountability, a Day of Judgment and even understandable terror as we stand before Almighty God.[35] The second is an unending joy that the all-consuming love of God has flung me out as an invitation for others to come to know Him. This invitation to know God is a double-edged sword. One edge is relationship with Him; the other is wrath for those who refuse the relationship. The invitation leaves nothing in existence between those two things. Relationship or wrath.

We must not live as if the intentions of God for us are unattainable, somehow impossible. We should not treat the written Word as if it is merely a compilation of suggestions that are only practical for pointing

---

[32] John 17:20-23

[33] Galatians 5:13

[34] Philippians 2:3

[35] 2 Corinthians 5:11

us in the direction in which to gaze. Since the goal of obedience eludes so many believers, they resign themselves to staying inside the moral boundaries that over-soft and accommodating preaching has created. Additionally, those very same anemic church attendees inadvertently exert demands for the very accommodations that hold them captive and upon the very teachers who accommodate them.[36]

Consider this parable that Jesus used to address this very issue in Luke 17:7-10 NLT:

"When a servant comes in from plowing or taking care of sheep, does his master say, 'Come in and eat with me'? No, he says, 'Prepare my meal, put on your apron, and serve me while I eat. Then you can eat later.' And does the master thank the servant for doing what he was told to do? Of course not. In the same way, when you obey me you should say, 'We are unworthy servants who have simply done our duty.' "

We do not have the option to hide behind the gracious love of God, whining on about how, "God knows my heart. He understands that I cannot really do the things commanded in the Bible." When we stand before God, He is not going to be interested in the desire of our heart. He is going to be interested in what we did or did not do.[37]

Of course, it is undeniably true that our works do not save us, but the Bible does talk about the importance of works. So what kind of works are these? Some theologians and preachers have attempted to convince us that no action whatsoever is involved in an individual's relationship with God. But look again at the Scripture. It says that we are God's workmanship, created for *good works* in Christ.[38] We are not

---

[36] 2 Timothy 4:3-4

[37] Matthew 25:31-46

[38] Ephesians 2:10

saved by self-works. But if we are truly saved, there will be good works in our lives, for that is our created purpose. Good works. God works. And faith without them is dead.[39]

I believe that if you have no power for obedience, then it follows that there isn't much presence of God in your life. Power for obedience starts with a decision to surrender to Jesus. Obedience to the whole will of God is not an option if you want to please God. Neither is it the final goal.

How is it that the faith of a Gentile astounded Jesus? (See Matthew 8:5-13.) The Bible says that the faith of the centurion astonished Jesus; it literally means astounded, caught off guard, surprised. Jesus was caught off guard by this foreigner's faith. How could this be? In Luke 8:40-48 there is another example:

Jesus was making His way through a throng of people when suddenly He stopped and turned to His disciples and asked, "Who touched Me?" A woman came forward and confessed. She had been sick for twelve years, and out of desperation, she had touched the hem of Jesus' robe. Her faith—faith that caught Jesus by surprise—drew healing power out of Him. He did not choose to release the healing; it was drawn out of Him by this lady's faith.

How is it possible that Jesus did not know who had done this? I'm not sure I fully understand this, but I do want my faith to sneak up on Jesus and surprise Him, drawing out His power to work extraordinary things! So how might this happen?

When the disciples were told by Jesus in Matthew 14:22-32 to get into a boat and cross to the other side of a lake without Him, they did as He told them. They were obedient. So far, so good. Simply doing what He tells us to do is the very least that we can do to be considered one of His disciples. Isn't that what we spend much of our time and

---

[39] James 2:17

effort and energy doing in our churches, trying to help people be obedient to Jesus? So then, what is the point of the parable of the servant in Luke 17 if merely obeying Jesus is our only goal?

The disciples encountered a storm late that night when they got far out onto the lake and they were afraid. That's exactly what may happen to us when we do as Jesus says. We may encounter storms and darkness and fear. Then Jesus will always come at the darkest hour if we are in the place that obedience has put us. That is what He did then. He came walking on top of the water to meet His disciples. His arrival scared them, just like it often does to us when Jesus truly shows up!

Peter looked at Jesus walking on top of the water and something happened inside his heart. *Possibility* seized him, and an idea of extraordinary proportions birthed inside his spirit. He first verified that it was really Jesus walking on the water, and then he asked if he could get out of the boat and go to Him. Jesus said yes.

Jesus will always tell us yes, if it is to Him that we want to come.

Peter got out of the boat and started to walk on the water to Jesus, then he got distracted by the problem at hand, took his eyes off Jesus, and started to sink. I have heard preachers all my life describe this as Peter's failure. I disagree. It was not a failure! The Bible says that he *started* to sink. How do you *start* to sink? Have you ever jumped in a swimming pool and *started* to sink? Never! You sink...period! The Bible does not say how far down he went. It could have been only enough to cover his feet. How is that a failure?

Okay, so now Peter is wading on the lake—that's still incredible! Being submerged a few inches is not much less of a miracle than walking on top! Even if Peter was knee deep or waist deep, still he was kept from sinking by *something*. I am talking about reaction time here! My point is that there had to be some continuing miraculous action with the physics in the water to give Peter time enough to get his eyes back on Jesus, cry out for help, and grab ahold of Jesus' hand.

A Sinking Experience

Audrey and I have quite an ongoing discussion about Peter's attempt to surf without a board. She thinks, pragmatically, that every action has a beginning point; therefore it is possible that when the Bible says Peter started to sink that that was the instant of the beginning of his going under. While she is, of course, theoretically correct—every action does have a beginning—I know from a real life experience that when the surface you are walking on suddenly and without notice changes form, there is indeed no time to do anything but sink. Here's my story:

When I was a new missionary I went to a service that was a drive of several hours from our house. I was still very inexperienced and this was one of the first services I had attended by myself. While there, the meal we ate included some very tough, grass fed beef. I had a gap between two of my teeth, and some of that hard, stringy meat got jammed near my gum.

At our staff meeting earlier that month David Hogan had held up a toothpick and told us that all experienced missionaries carried a toothpick with them. I didn't take him too seriously. After all, I'm a country boy and I can pick a stalk of grass to pick my teeth if I need to.

Now, by the end of the normal three-hour-long church service, my gum was throbbing. Using my fingernail and my tongue, I *could not* get that piece of meat out for anything. I still had a three-hour drive ahead of me and my gum was pounding! I thought that surely I had the fortitude to make the drive home where I knew the toothpicks awaited to work a wondrous deliverance to the throbbing pain in my mouth.

I made it all the way to the outskirts of my town but just could not handle the discomfort and pain any longer. So I pulled over at the first location I felt comfortable with since it was so late at night. I could almost feel the bulge in my gum through my cheek! I had waited all of that time and distance to be sure and stop in a safe place and chose a gas station I went to all the time. I drove to the end of the pavement and put the truck in neutral and put on the emergency brake.

Now, I grew up out in the country in rural Alabama, and what you did if you needed to pick your teeth was grab a piece of grass or straw and "have at it."

Well, relying upon prior knowledge and experience that had never failed me before, I spotted, in the light of my headlights, the perfect tooth-picking grass stem, the kind with the round, straw-like stalks, with a joint. It's at the joint that if you pull just right the stalk slides out, and in your hand you hold the best toothpick that money could buy.

I zeroed in on that perfect knee-high grass stalk, expertly selecting it from countless thousands of others. As I neared the object of my imminent dental relief, suddenly the ground disappeared from beneath my feet! *What in the world!* I instantly found myself hanging by my elbows on the edges of a sewage manhole. Not just any sewage, mind you, but green, slimy, stinky, fermented sewage. Who knew where the bottom might be!

The Lord helped me catch myself, and somehow my outstretched elbows prevented me from sinking. My observation is that I did not "start to sink." I immediately sank up to my waist. I had no time to think, much less holler for help. I had no time to reach for anyone. I only realized what had happened to me after I was somehow standing back on solid ground having sprung myself back to safety by leveraging my elbows and arms.

My point is that if I had not had help by the intervention of *something*, I would have sunk under water before my brain could even register what was happening!

So back to the story about Peter—something had to give him the time to have the presence of mind to ask for help! He called out and immediately Jesus *reached out His hand* and pulled him back to the surface. Peter got within an arm's length of Jesus! Then they apparently walked to the boat together. Obedience was the thing that positioned Peter for the opportunity to do this extraordinary thing. This was no failure!

Jesus did rebuke Peter for doubting. He said, "You of little faith, why did you doubt?" Always when I'd heard this story taught the preacher would key on the "little faith" statement, highlighting that it was the smallness of Peter's faith that was the culprit. I don't think this is what Jesus was emphasizing.

He could have just said, "*Peter*, why did you doubt?" It actually was Peter's little faith that got him out of the boat—that allowed him to walk on water in the first place. The problem was not the amount of faith that Peter had. Jesus did not say anything about him getting more faith or having more doubt. The equation in this story was constant: Peter got out of the boat with a certain amount of faith and a certain amount of doubt. The only difference in walking and starting to sink is how those two things interacted with each other. The thing that started him on his way under the water was the fact that he allowed doubt to climb on top of his faith and *begin* to push him down. He took his eyes off Jesus and put them on the problem surrounding him.

As I've noted earlier, I spent many years of my life trying to banish doubt and get enough faith to succeed. Now I know that we all have enough faith to do anything. I also know that doubt exists inside each of us, and the reality is that it is impossible to banish. Faith and doubt are in a constant wrestling match, and what I think Jesus was questioning Peter about was why he had let doubt get the upper hand on his faith. When he got out of the boat and began walking on the water his faith had the upper hand.

When Peter saw Jesus walking on the water toward the boat, something happened inside of him. The question I have is, "Whose idea was it for Peter to get out of the boat?"

I think it was Peter's idea. That is how the Bible records it. It does not say that Jesus told Peter to get out of the boat. It is written that way for a reason. There are no mistakes in the way the Bible is written. When he saw Jesus, he was inspired to do something impossible. At that point Peter exceeded basic obedience. All the things that he had heard Jesus teach, and all of the things that he had seen Him do, came together in that moment and he did something, inspired by Jesus, that was *extraordinary*.

When he saw Jesus, he was inspired to do something impossible.

That has become one of my goals—*to exceed obedience.* I believe that is without a doubt the surest way we get to hear the words, "Well done, good and faithful servant! Come and share your master's happiness."[40]

And by the way, when I got home—my slimy stinky self—Audrey helped me strip out of the sewage-soaked pants I was wearing and took off my nasty boots and hurried me off to the shower. She also brought me a beautiful, round, manufactured toothpick. With one delicate thrust, the meat was gone and my gum found relief!

I carry toothpicks now.

---

[40] Matthew 25:21,23

---

1 5

Your Little Is Enough

Do you sometimes feel inadequate? I do.

Often I have thought that if I were more talented or had the abilities I see in others, I could do a better job in what Jesus has called me to do. More times than not, I have felt scared and inadequate, trapped in the suspension between seeing so much of what could be accomplished and the lack of the substance necessary to carry out what God's told me to do.

I have been told that I am a lateral thinker in some things, meaning that without much processing I can draw conclusions intuitively that oftentimes end up being correct. I see so many things rapidly from start to finish, and sometimes I am frustrated with my inability to convey that to the people around me. I see the goal clearly, and yet I also see why someone else would be better suited to attempt what I know needs to be accomplished.

Take writing this book for instance. I had no interest in writing a book, but Jesus spoke to me and told me to write, so I wrote. All through grammar school, and even into high school, I was labeled as learning disabled. I was always behind in school and felt lost and panicked at never having my assignments done on time. I was placed in special education classes and treated as if I could not learn.

I have dyslexia, which has caused me to struggle with traditional learning. My type of dyslexia does not manifest itself as much in reversing letters and words as it does in preventing me from seeing patterns in numbers. It clogs my thinking when things are presented to me as two-dimensional ideas. I see things in pictures, and my brain wants to turn everything into a three-dimensional object. It processes thousands of times more than the brain of people who do not think in three dimensions, and that makes me tired, not wanting to engage in the thinking process. With English grammar, my brain just could not figure out how to deal with abstract concepts like parts of speech, and it tried to make three-dimensional objects out of a language structure that is riddled with exceptions.

I did not really learn to read well until I was in the eighth grade. My brother gave me an illustrated edition of *The Hobbit*, which I was willing to try to read because it had pictures. It was the first book that I read from cover to cover. Something happened to me during that process. I made the discovery, late at night, of reading on my own, struggling to sound out so many new words. I saw that there was a way to turn two dimensions into three. The two-dimensional words became a movie in my mind. Oh, the worlds that open up when one begins to read!

I struggled in high school English, barely able to pass each class. As I wrote any of the required papers, or even letters to friends or family, my brain didn't know how to translate the living world in my head onto the flat prison of a piece of paper. I was lost in mathematics, but English grammar defied reason!

In the tenth grade I was sitting in a special-ed class when a substitute teacher, Linda Hill, noticed something about me that all my other teachers hadn't. She was the advanced placement history teacher for our Pinson Valley High School. Somehow Mrs. Hill recognized that I was probably not learning disabled, but that I was bored because of some mental processing challenges.

She invited me to join her AP history class. Considering my academic record, I was shocked. Never had a teacher who dealt with gifted and smart people ever given me any serious consideration. When she asked me into her AP class it changed my whole mental outlook on school and learning. She told me I could do whatever I set my mind to. She found the things that I could do well and adjusted her teaching to reflect the ways I could learn better.

As if a switch had been flipped, my brain began to function in a way that allowed me to excel in that class. I never made below a ninety-five on any exam she gave. My mother had always told me, and all of my skeptical teachers, that I was not a slow learner and was not dumb. After Mrs. Hill took an interest in me and brought me into her world, other teachers joined in preparing me for college. Their attitude became "you can" instead of "you probably never will."

This environment now matched my home environment and set me up positively for success in school. I won the Woodmen of the World history award that year for the highest academic performance in that AP history class! This was something unprecedented in my life, unthinkable until one teacher saw something in me that others had missed.

This is a great lesson for all of us, to always be looking for the "truth" of people based on how God created them.

I was accepted without problem into Auburn University. It was the only school that I applied to. That is amazing to me, because there was a time when I thought I would barely make it through high school.

While at Auburn studying wildlife biology, I met Audrey. She was the opposite of me academically, truly one of the smartest people I have ever met. Learning came easy for her. She has a gift for writing and actually *understands* English grammar! She also has a gift for teaching and has used that gift with our children and me.

If I have any ability to order my thoughts and lay them down with any clarity on a page, it is because Audrey spent countless hours helping me calm down the chaos in my head enough to let coherency express itself through my pen. (However, all of her most gifted attempts to teach me how to spell have failed miserably. Thank You, Jesus, for spell-check!)

I am relating this part of my story to make a point about our spiritual growth. We see our own weaknesses and spend much energy pleading with God to alleviate them. Moses did the same thing when God summoned him out of the desert and charged him with the awesome task of leading the Israelites out of Egypt. He argued with God until God got mad at him. Moses based his argument on his own limitations compared to the enormity of the task he was commissioned to carry out.

He told God something (Exodus 4:10) that is both very interesting and encouraging to me. Moses explained to God that he could not speak well, neither before he met God nor afterward. God left him with his *inability*, all the while asking him to do something that he was bad at. Moses would have preferred that God fix his problem, but God did not fix his problem, He used Moses *with* his problem.

Moses had the burning bush experience that so many of us desire. Yet encounter with God did not erase his weakness.[41]

Gideon had a similar experience when God chose him to work a great deliverance for the nation of Israel. Gideon explained to God that he was from the least tribe in Israel and from the least family in that tribe. God left Gideon's position intact, even as he moved Gideon out of perceived limitations and brought a great victory for His people.[42]

---

[41] Exodus 4:10

[42] Judges 6:11-23

When the disciples recognized the problem of feeding five thousand men plus women and children in a desolate place, they approached Jesus and offered their man-wisdom solution to the situation. Jesus had a different plan. "They don't need to go away," He said, "*you* give them something to eat." When He said that, they responded out of their limited resources, "We only have five loaves of bread and two fish!"

"Then bring me the little you have."[43]

That is exactly the point: Jesus can do anything! Bring Jesus the little you have and He will bless it and give it back, and you will see astonishing things flow from your own hands.

> Bring Jesus the little you have and He will bless it and give it back, and you will see astonishing things flow from your own hands.

Your little is enough!

When I was approached about writing this book, it was the furthest thing from my mind. There was no way I could write a book! In my mind I still saw myself through the grid of the dismal failure of my high school English term papers. Besides, I believe we already may have too many books written in the church. We certainly do not need another excuse for people not to have to seek God for themselves.

I detest the merchandising that has turned the church into a den of thieves. Religious snake oil salesmen prostitute their persuasive gifts for monetary gain. I would rather break all my teeth out eating rocks than be associated with any of these people.

Only the direction of Jesus forced me to embrace this writing task.

May this book not be anything other than a tool to draw you toward Jesus.

---

[43] Matthew 14:16-18

God wants to use the little we have to accomplish extraordinary things. He fully intends to use us as we are, with our inabilities intact, to accomplish His will on this earth. For it is through our weakness that His power is made perfect.[44] It is our weakness that helps reveal the greatness of God. We want God to do away with our deficiency, but God leaves it in place so that others can clearly see His power at work in us.

If God were to alleviate our weaknesses and inabilities, then others would see our perfection instead of God's power. He asks the impossible of us. He requires faith because faith leads to extraordinary things, and only God can accomplish truly extraordinary things. We have everything we need now to move forward with what He has commissioned us to do.

———————

Yet fear traps so many of us. We forget that many of our heroes in the Bible struggled with fear, too. We think that if we can just have a dramatic encounter with God, then we will turn into someone we are not, able to leap over every obstacle with ease.

Most of the time we are crawling, not leaping, over obstacles. Some sit dumbfounded staring at the height of the obstacle. Or they cower in fear, focused on the crippled state of their legs instead of looking at the One who created the universe.

God has told Moses, Gideon, the disciples, and us: "I am sending you. I will be with you. Do not fear. These signs will accompany you. *Go!*" I can't recall God calling anyone in the Bible to do anything amazing if He did not also give them His miraculous power to accomplish the task—not in the Old Testament, not in the New Testament, and not today. Why would He change things now?

---

[44] 2 Corinthians 12:9

God does not change. God *has not* changed.[45] He will use you and me to do extraordinary and miraculous things, with the limitations and lack of abilities that we have *right now*. It's not about us. It's about Him. The little we have is enough.

Trust Him. Believe Him. Seek Him with all your being, without preconditions, for the rest of your life and just see what happens.

Just do it! Just move out and begin. Use what you know and what you've been given. Stop your endless learning and training without action, waiting on God to change your inadequacies into abilities before you begin doing what you know He wants you to do.

You may have been waiting on God for years, not realizing that God is waiting on *you*. You are searching as hard as you can for God to write instructions on a wall with a giant hand. Do you really want the handwriting on the wall? The last guy who got a message like that died that very night of the judgment that the message announced.[46]

> I can't recall God calling anyone in the Bible to do anything amazing if He did not also give them His miraculous power to accomplish the task— not in the Old Testament, not in the New Testament, and not today.

When the children of Israel crossed the Jordan River for the first time as a nation to take possession of the Promised Land God worked a mighty miracle. The river piled up in both directions in a heap, stopped by the hand of God in midair. The people walked over to the

---

[45] Hebrews 13:8

[46] Daniel 5

other bank on dry ground, but the river did not part until the priests got their feet completely into the water.[47]

Maybe you have tried to move out, only to be confronted with failure. You decided to dip your little toe in the river instead of committing with all your spirit, soul, and body because you were thinking of your recovery plan in case things didn't work out.

Just like the Israelites, we have to get completely into the water, totally committed, before the miraculous power will begin to flow. So many believers who love God only dabble with committing their whole life to the fulfillment of the Great Commission.

Before the miracles started happening in our ministry I prayed and prayed for many people who were sick and afflicted, and very few of them got healed. But it was not until I was fully committed to our church planting process that the supernatural power really began to flow through us.

It does not matter what your career may be. Everybody is commanded to win souls, make disciples, and advance the Kingdom of God. We falsely assume that this activity is a matter of being called to "full-time ministry." It's estimated that there are three billion people alive today who do not have access to anyone in their life who is able to share the Gospel with them. This is not a matter of calling. It is a command. Reaching the lost is a command given to every one of us. Engage where you are. Calling has to do with *where* you obey this command, not *if* you obey it.

The proof that we love Jesus is that we keep His commands, not that we merely have an emotional attachment to our microcosmic church culture.[48]

Jesus *commands* us to go!

GO! In God's hands, your little is enough!

---

[47] Joshua 3:8

[48] John 14:15

16

Relationship

God has gone to great lengths to provide a pathway for us to reunite with Him in fellowship, both now in this life and for eternity. God the Father wants us to walk and talk with Him now, in preparation for the relationship we will have with Him forever.

God sent His Son, Jesus, to become a man, suffer hunger and thirst, pain and bliss, joy and heartache, and finally, to voluntarily lay down His life for us. His death opened the door for relationship with God to all who will accept His sacrifice. The reason for His death is so we can have what Adam had with God in the Garden before the fall of mankind.

When we do not cultivate a personal and living relationship, walking with God, talking with God, living as He wants us to live, and seeing what He wants us to see, we are trampling on the blood of the Lamb.

We must seek Jesus. He is real. He is alive. He interacts with people as He did with those we know of from the New Testament. If that is not the Jesus you experience, I urge you to seek Him with all of your being. You will find Him![49]

---

[49] Jeremiah 29:10-14

The narrow road of Christ cannot be widened. We must determine not to misapply our compassion to people struggling with the demands of discipleship in an attempt to make a four-lane road out of a narrow footpath. If we delve into this line of reasoning, we will inadvertently propagate a way of the Cross that has no power.[50]

Such a life also becomes relationshipless. This no longer is the way of the Gospel of the Lord Jesus Christ. It becomes whatever a man comes up with through tampering with the truth by his imagined "right of private interpretation."

Modern fads have recently swept through the church and have sold the softening and obscuring of the truth. We are pressured to focus on "seekers" rather than on God. The Cross gets downplayed, or ignored altogether, so "seekers" won't be offended. We are instructed not to allow the Holy Spirit to make an appearance in our main services, but rather hide Him in a side room or small group. We are told not to mention sin or hell, or maybe just promote a heresy that says sin does not exist because we are under grace. Human wisdom pushes cultural relevance as the new paradigm to modernize the message and make it "relevant" to "seekers". The plain spoken and blunt truth has been cowed and gagged by this repackaged religious political correctness. All these things have led me to believe that the spirit of the age is trying to push through a "new spiritual renaissance," but there is no such thing as a "new spiritual renaissance." It is just the sad, dull, humanistic trappings of institutional Christianity, repackaged and regurgitated through the fads of cultural relevance.

There is nothing new under the sun.[51]

---

[50] 1 Corinthians 1:17

[51] Ecclesiastes 1:9

Our life in Jesus is not intended to be about religion or religious practices. It is about relationship. Jesus is alive and He has not changed.[52] What Jesus used to do, He still does now. He is not soft and accommodating in His love for us. For our own good, He is blunt and hard and crushing to our sinful nature. He is unrelenting and exclusive in His pursuit of us.[53] He paid the ultimate price for His intention to save us from ourselves: death on a cross.[54]

All things in the Kingdom are about knowing God. He is jealous and will not ultimately tolerate any other devotion in our hearts except our devotion to Him and what is linked to that.[55] To know Him is to obey Him. In order to obey Him, we must follow His Son. Following His Son means doing what He did, thinking as He thought, and living like He lived. This is possible but difficult, and it differs from the common picture we have created of what following Christ looks like. Indeed, I believe in many cases we have reduced Christianity into a mere religion.

Religions are ordered collections of thoughts and philosophies, ideas of men about spiritual, social, mental, and civil conduct. There are many such religions, and there will likely be more created by brilliantly deceived humans.

To associate Jesus with religion is to try to fit Him into the same putrid categories of other ideas, hoping He somehow comes out on top. Jesus is not an idea. He is not a philosophy. *He is.* It was by Him that God made all things. Jesus lives. He is the Son of Almighty God. He is all-consuming, and to attempt to compare Jesus in any category to anything or anybody else places us in danger of eternal damnation. He is beyond compare.

---

[52] Hebrews 13:8

[53] Romans 9:33, 1 Peter 2:8, Matthew 21:44, Luke 11:23

[54] Philippians 2:8

[55] Exodus 20:1-6

The invitation to know Jesus is the most extraordinary truth of all. It is the reason Jesus laid down His life on the Cross. It is the thing that drives our commission as His ambassadors on this earth. Yet we blindly, foolishly, incomprehensibly, and sometimes selfishly, ignore Him.

I hear the echo of these words God has burned into my heart:

"For my people have done two evil things: They have abandoned me—the fountain of living water. And they have dug for themselves cracked cisterns that can hold no water at all!" (Jeremiah 2:13 NLT).

I hear God saying:

I have sent them My Scripture so they can understand how to come to Me. I have sent My Spirit to draw them back to Me and to give them new cisterns, new wineskins. What have My people found wrong with Me that they run from Me and, instead, run after themselves? They prostitute themselves on the wide road that includes everything except Me! If they do not accept the new wineskin, then the new wine will cause them destruction.[56]

Beyond that, I hear the Lord saying:

Your effectiveness in Me is wrapped up in what you worship. When you worship worthless idols, you become worthless yourself.[57] *I love My people and am drawing them close by an open show of My power, to shout to them that they have filled their lives with the worship of themselves, with the worship of worthless things—things made by man, things that trap and distract them. Why? I want them to come to Me. Can they not see that I AM?*

I come to the garden searching for them, and when they hear Me coming they run and hide. Sin has corrupted their hearts even though I have plainly shown them the way. The servants whom I

---

[56] Mark 2:22

[57] Psalm 115:1-8

have sent to them, who are teaching My Word, have ignored Me themselves, mistakenly thinking that the Scriptures give eternal life. I am Life, but they refuse to come to Me to have life.

I told them to teach My people to obey My commands, yet they spend all their resources and talents on only teaching the commands. So My people remain powerless to put into practice what I expect of them. I brought them the fruits of abundance, and they have corrupted the land of plenty I have given them. Why? Why won't they come to Me?

I have been consumed with finding God for as long as I can remember. It is the angle from which I live. It is the angle from which I interpret the Scripture. It is the angle that moves me in making disciples. Without Him, I can do nothing.[58]

The very essence of why Jesus died is so that we can have a relationship with God. It is why we were created. Jesus is the bridge that spans the unbridgeable gulf that sin drove between God and mankind.

If we are not people who burn with this singular purpose of knowing Him personally and helping others to know Him, then we are in effect saying that the death of Jesus means nothing.

Jesus is constantly knocking on the door of our life, daily asking to come in (Revelation 3:20). We must answer that knock every day. We must walk with Him every day. The Blood of our Master was poured out on the Cross so that we can enjoy the privilege of opening this fellowship door with the Son of God.

I urge you to take advantage of the opportunity to open that door daily! There is no message that has more importance than that. There is no function that has more urgency than that. There is no purpose that is more dominant than that. Everything in our life must come from this.

---

[58] Isaiah 26:12, John 15:5

If we don't enter gladly and deeply into this relationship, are we not treating the sacrifice that Jesus made on the Cross with contempt?

Just because you feel you have entrusted yourself to Jesus does not mean He has entrusted Himself to you.

Exactly what does it mean to know Jesus? Is it becoming increasingly aware of the operation of supernatural gifts? Is it the presence of God-given talents? Is it the fact that you may be in so-called full-time ministry? Is it the reality that you live a good moral life and participate in good citizenship?

I believe, sadly, that many who believe they are saved really do not know Jesus. Be honest. Is your life like what is described and demonstrated in the Bible? Are you living as Jesus wants you to? If you are saved, Jesus knows you, but how intimate are you with Him? Just because you feel you have entrusted yourself to Jesus does not mean He has entrusted Himself to you. Here's what Scripture says about this:

> Now while he was in Jerusalem at the Passover Feast, many people saw the miraculous signs he was doing and believed in his name. But Jesus would not entrust himself to them, for he knew all men (John 2:23-24).

Jesus will entrust Himself to us if we will determine to work towards walking in fellowship with Him every day. But we must prove ourselves faithful to the relationship with Him that He has given to us.

The Apostle Paul wrote this:

> So then, men ought to regard us as servants of Christ and as those entrusted with the secret things of God. Now it is

required that those who have been given a trust must prove faithful (1 Corinthians 4:1-2).

What exactly is God looking for in order for us to prove ourselves faithful so that Jesus will entrust Himself to us? Faithfulness will always bring you to the place where God will begin to move in your life. It is oftentimes the most difficult thing to execute over the whole of your life. But faithfulness and consistency are the character traits most important for lifelong spiritual longevity.

Being born again means a lifelong dedication to the presence of God, the things of God, and the service of God on this earth. In return we look forward to spending eternity in His presence in His Kingdom. Getting born again is the end of one life and purpose, and the beginning of a new life and purpose. To be saved means total dedication to God. And once we get saved, we start to worship God.

Those are the two essential ingredients: lifelong dedication and worship.

What does your secret life consist of? Are you defined by the presence of God? How much do you pray? How much do you fast? Most importantly, how often do you worship God? How many people have you witnessed to as a result of what God is doing in your life because of your worship of Him? Are you making disciples? Do you regularly pray for the sick in person?

If these things are not consistent, then there can be no surety that God will come to you in the night as He did with Samuel, and call you by name...and change your universe.[59]

You may feel that such a life lived for Jesus is unattainable. It is not! We are the temple of the Holy Spirit, destined to be carriers of the presence of God to the ends of the earth. That is why when Jesus died the curtain of the temple was torn in half. Now we are the carriers. God's

---

[59] 1 Samuel 3

glory is no longer confined in a building made with the hands of men. He decided to dwell inside temples that live and move.

You must lay down your life.[60] Sell out! Do not faint. Have endurance. Jesus will send His Spirit to help you.[61] It is to this end that He is bringing us. He earnestly desires to reveal Himself to us in this way. Jump in! Begin this process with God. We must respond to Him, for this is why He died.

Jesus said that we must be born again.[62] This draws a comparison to our natural life. Indeed, our natural life reflects the reality of the unseen world. Because Jesus used this comparison, let's look at it more closely.

When a baby is born, what is the most critical health concern for that baby at birth? Breathing. The attending doctor is not first concerned about whether the baby wants something to eat or drink. He wants to know if the newborn is breathing. Breathing is the most critical thing we do as far as moment-by-moment living. If you cannot breathe, nothing else matters.

The second most critical thing we do is drinking. If we are severely dehydrated, we don't think about food, nor do we have the ability to eat.

The third most critical thing we do is eating. Without nourishment there is no energy to function and no basis for growth. We can live a few minutes without air, a few days without water, and forty days or so without food.

In these three things we see the basic ingredients for life—breathing, drinking, and eating. Since this natural life parallels our spiritual

---

[60] Luke 9:23

[61] John 14:15-17

[62] John 3:3

life, what are the three comparable ingredients at the spiritual level? Since breath determines viability at birth, what determines spiritual viability when a person gets born again? It is prayer.[63] You cannot get born again without communicating with God; therefore it follows that since that is the first thing you do during a new birth, prayer is your spiritual breath.

Jesus also promised to place within us rivers of living water.[64] This is the Holy Spirit. Without the filling of the Holy Spirit, spiritual dehydration follows.

Finally, the written Word is our food.[65] From it comes all our spiritual nourishment and strength.

We should live our life with all of this in mind. We should pray, so we are not gasping to death. We should be full of the Holy Spirit so we have something to drink and avoid dehydration. And we should read the Bible, all of it, cover to cover, on a continual basis, so that we can grow.

I know many people who faithfully read and study the Bible who aren't equally devoted to prayer and worship; but I don't know anyone who consistently seeks God through prayer and worship who is not devoted to the Bible.

First things must be first. Prayer and worship cause filling to happen. Prayer and worship are the platform from which all things spring. Seek God with all your heart, with all your mind, and with all your strength.[66] If you do not faint, one day or night, Jesus will come to you, having decided that you are trustworthy with His presence, and He will personally call you by name.

Nothing else can compare to this relationship!

---

[63] Romans 10:9

[64] John 7:38-39

[65] 1 Corinthians 3:2, Hebrews 5:11-14

[66] Deuteronomy 4:29, Jeremiah 29:13, Luke 10:27

1 7

Walking with Jesus

Everywhere Audrey goes she impacts people for Jesus. Whether it is in a remote village among countless other hidden villages, at the grocery store in the United States, at the mall, or in a church, she is constantly praying for people, talking with people, and leading people to Jesus. She is a true Jesus-follower, and she makes Jesus attractive to people everywhere she goes. Here's one story out of hundreds she could tell.

Sunday is market day. The streets are closed to traffic and people from different villages gather to buy and sell. One day I walked to the market with my colorful woven plastic market bags to buy food for our family for the week. The market was filled with the wonderful colors of varied fruits and vegetables. Fresh meat hung from hooks in the small meat shops. Piles of plucked chickens on small wooden tables were cut with sharp machetes and sold. The chicken feet were sold at a good price.

People sat on steps and on the sidewalk selling their wares. Vendors called out their prices for shoes and belts, grass sleeping mats and matches, underclothes and incense, flashlights and fish. Fresh steamed corn was put on a stick, slathered with mayonnaise, topped with freshly grated cheese and a final sprinkle of chili powder then sold as a special treat called elote. Handmade jewelry and hand-stitched shirts were on display and sold.

As I walked along making purchases I felt a hand on my arm and turned to see a tiny woman holding her hand out for a peso or two. Her hands and arms were so skinny—flesh draped on bone. My heart hurt for her. I gave her some money and she kissed me.

There are several regular beggars in our town, but this one particularly stayed in my mind. I wanted to buy her some food, give her something with substance.

> But Jesus...
>
> He offered her hope.
>
> Hope for the right
>
> now, and hope for the
>
> eternity to come.

The next week I saw her again and invited her to my house. I brought her home with me so that she would know where we live. That started a relationship. I found out her name was Maria, like so many others. In order to differentiate her from the others, our family affectionately called her Skinny Maria.

At times I saw her in town and bought her food from the market. At times she came to our house. She spoke Nahuatl, her native language, and didn't speak much Spanish, and my Spanish was not great at that time, but we communicated. Her life was miserable. She was hurting terribly. Her stomach ached all the time, and she had a hard time keeping food down. Her clothes were falling apart. Her husband and son had abandoned her. She had no means of support.

I told her that I understood her life was hard, but that without Jesus it would only get worse. Hell is a lot worse than even a terrible life here on earth. But Jesus...He offered her hope. Hope for the right now, and hope for the eternity to come. I had the privilege to tell Skinny Maria about the love of Jesus, and she decided to accept Him into her life.

I began to read the New Testament to her. This helped my Spanish so much and it fed her soul. Sometimes when I finished a chapter she wanted me to keep on reading. How beautiful.

Yes, it was a privilege to care for her, but sometimes I had to remind myself of that. Many times she would ring the doorbell right when I was in the middle of home schooling the kids or doing some other project. Sometimes I didn't feel like going downstairs and talking with her and listening to her problems. Then I would remind myself that this is really what we live for. Spelling could wait.

Hannah, Aspen, or I would fix her something to drink and try to convince her to eat something, and then I would read the Bible to her. Sometimes we raided our refrigerator and sent her home with tomatoes and onions and jalapenos. She was grateful.

One day she came to the house and opened the dirty bag she carried everywhere and pulled out a small plastic bag. She slowly and carefully unwrapped something she had wrapped in corn husks. She had brought me a gift—two beautiful brown eggs. Weeks earlier I had given her 200 pesos to buy some hens and corn feed. Now her chickens were laying eggs and she wanted to share with me. She gave me what she could in order to express her gratitude. I thanked her as she left and then I went upstairs and cried. I showed them to my family and our dear friends, Pastors Mark and Christie Marble, who had come to Mexico simply to visit and encourage us. Christie and I cried together at the enormity of those two small eggs.

I cry now as I think about it. The widow's mite was in my hand.

Time passed and our relationship grew. Another missionary family, Kenny and Christina Carter and their four children, moved to our town to work with us. I introduced them to Skinny Maria. Christina now had the opportunity to minister to her as well.

Some days Maria would go to Christina's house, some days to mine, and some days she went to both of us. A few times she was so weak I made a pallet on the floor and had her lay down and rest while I read to her.

One day I sat on the floor next to her and tried to massage her back where she showed me she was hurting. But how do you massage bone? She had so little flesh on her frame. It made me sad. I'm a mother to the core, so I comforted her as best I could. I rubbed her back and prayed for her, as I had so many times for my own children.

Week after week I read her the Bible. When I didn't see her for a while I got worried. Sometime before, I had asked her to show me where she lived so I could find her if there was an emergency. Britt and I took Pastors Mike and Kim Ewoldt, who were visiting from Hattiesburg, Mississippi, and we went to try and find her in her house of sticks and stones. We found her curled up on her bed of boards, hurting. I knelt by her and prayed for her and spoke to her about Jesus. When we left I thought she wouldn't live, but she did, so we continued to care for her.

Her green hand-me-down blazer that she used as a coat was falling apart so I sewed the seams back together. It was such a simple thing for me to do with my sewing machine. She was so grateful. One day I bought her a dress. We went to a lot of small shops to find just the one she wanted. She chose a little girl's pink party dress with roses sewn on the waistband. She took it home with her and never wore it. Her treasure.

Many days she left our house with a bucket, or a teacup, or a blanket. How could I not help her? Jesus told us to care for her, so we did. Sometimes I gave her money, and sometimes not. Sometimes I had a good attitude when she came by, and sometimes not. But we didn't abandon her. She became very special to us. We read all the way to 2 Corinthians together.

Then one day Maria didn't come by. She had died. I was sad and yet relieved for her. She made it to Heaven. She had Jesus as her Savior and she no longer hurt. Now she could sit at the banquet feast with Jesus and eat and be filled. The rain didn't leak through a tarpaper roof in Heaven. She was not abandoned, but embraced. She was not outcast, but brought near.

My life is full of Marias.

Yours is too.

1 8

Take Off Your Sandals

Of all the things that we can fall prey to in our journey with Christ, the mixing of our own knowledge and wisdom with God's is the most difficult to recognize and the most dangerous. Embedded in our nature is the tendency to try to usurp God's throne. We seem to constantly struggle to determine the proper boundaries for everything.

If we closely examine the fall of Lucifer and compare it with the fall of mankind, we discover a chilling common denominator.

In Isaiah 14 we read of the ultimate corruption of one of God's most beautiful and powerful beings. Rebellion was born in the heart of Lucifer, and he became saturated with jealousy to usurp God. The ultimate position the "son of the dawn" could imagine was to be like God Himself: "I will make myself like the Most High" (verse 14). This was Lucifer's downfall.

In Genesis, Satan, in the body of a serpent, tempted Eve and all of mankind with this identical, feverish idea: "And you will be like God" (Genesis 3:5). The enemy of our soul is obsessed with this idea, and so it was that the same weakness that caused Lucifer's downfall caused our own.

Throughout the ages mankind has struggled with this very practice. God speaks over and over of obedience, surrender, laying down our life, and drinking the bitter cup. All these things have to do with us bowing to Him. He is our Lord. All of our daily and eternal problems arise from struggling against this fact.

Early in the recorded history of the redeemed, we find within the children of God the ugly reality of humanistic self-supremacy attempting to take pieces of His deity. In the book of Exodus we see the people of God in the wilderness, waiting for Moses to come down the mountain after his meeting with God. The people demanded that their temporary leader, Aaron, make an image for God—the Almighty God who had led them out of Egypt. They were not crafting a new god. They were simply taking things into their own hands and giving the God who had delivered them their own definition of what they thought He should look like, what He should consist of, and what His dimensions ought to be. They wanted something that they could see and touch and understand, defined by their own limited boundaries.

Aaron gave in to their demands and said, "Tomorrow there will be a festival to the LORD" (Exodus 32:5). He did not call this image by a new and foreign name. He called it Yahweh, the LORD, the One who had brought them out of Egypt with such dramatic power. The people were clearly trying to mix the divine with the human. We also see that Aaron was designating a festival to God. So the next day the people offered sacrifices and offerings to God. After that they ate and got up to indulge the flesh.

God then spoke to Moses and told him to go to the people because they had "become corrupt" (Exodus 32:7). What was the corruption? What had made God so mad that He wanted to destroy them all? Was it not the same attitude of rebellion that caused Lucifer and mankind to fall in the first place?

Let's examine what happened.

Whose idea was it to have festivals of worship to the Lord? It was God's idea. Whose idea was it to give Jehovah an image to worship?

Man's. Whose idea was it to offer burnt and fellowship offerings? God's. Whose idea was it to indulge in revelry? Man's. Can you see how what these people did was mix the wisdom of God with the wisdom of man? God hates that.

Temptation opened Adam and Eve's eyes, and they were made aware of the existence of a wisdom that was not from God: "When the woman saw that the fruit of the tree was good for food and pleasing to the eye, and also desirable for gaining *wisdom*, she took some and ate it" (Genesis 3:6, emphasis added). Eve dined on the wisdom of the world—human wisdom, and it was the mixing of human wisdom with the wisdom of God that made God so angry. In His eyes it was a detestable corruption that those whom He had claimed as His own would attempt to use their own human ideas mixed with His.

––––––

The fact that God hates the mixing of man ideas with His ideas is plainly stated when He forbade the Israelites to shape the stones of His altar: "If you make an altar of stones for me, do not build it with dressed stones, for you will *defile* it if you use a tool on it" (Exodus 20:25, emphasis added). When we touch the things of God in an attempt to add definition to them and make them more pleasing or familiar or relevant to us, we defile them. Is your "spirit of excellence" in order to glorify God or merely an excuse for shaping stones so that they look good to *you*? Yes, we should do all things to the best of our ability, but we must follow Him and not preempt God with our own ideas of what we think is pleasing to Him.[67]

Above all, the goal should be to build the altar that *He* desires, from *His* design, and at *His* direction. If the Lord does not build a house, he

---

[67] 1 Corinthians 1:27

who builds labors in vain (Psalm 127:1a). God gave very specific instructions and wanted shaped stones for Solomon's Temple.[68] For His own altar He wanted natural stone not altered by man.[69] The point isn't how they look, but rather listening to hear what He says. The point is that Jesus is LORD.

I love the local church. I love how varied the Body of Christ is around the world. I love big churches with multiple thousands of people in big buildings. I love a church of ten people meeting in a hut with colored sheets of plastic for walls. I love pastors who wear shirts with embroidered eagles and pointed elf shoes, and barefoot pastors who can't read. Not one way is right. Jesus is right. We should listen to Him and respond to His voice. When we go into villages we dress in simple clothes so as to not further distance ourselves from the people since we are already so different. Observe. Listen. Respond.

The defilement occurs when we follow a vision God's given us but use our own definition of what carrying out that vision looks like.

I don't want to sound critical of the church. Reach the people in the best way you can so that they can truly hear the message and see the power of God. The way you dress and the way you talk will open or close doors. Be aware of the culture so as not to offend people, but don't think that the power of God is dependent on that. I have spoken to thousands of young people in my Wal-Mart jeans and western shirt and they listened and then responded to the move of the Holy Spirit. It's Jesus, not the jeans.

---

[68] I Kings 6:7

[69] Exodus 20:25, Deuteronomy 27:5

Please hear my heart. If He says, "Shape the stones," then you should shape the stones. If He says, "Leave it natural," then leave it natural. The defilement occurs when we follow a vision God's given us but use our own definition of what carrying out that vision looks like.

Where does the inspiration for what you do come from? Church growth seminars? People you are working with? Did you go to God for your instruction or go to a successful pastor and try to apply what worked for him in your own field? Is it pressure from the people in your church? You can gain wisdom from others, but don't let that be your all in all. Go to God.

In the Old Testament the altar was the place to meet with God and to determine our acceptability to Him. It was where the divine and human met, and the doorway was established for interaction between the two.

What does the altar of God signify for us today? I often see in America that we have the most beautifully shaped and adorned altars of any church on earth. Yet the way that many churches do ministry is shaped with layer upon layer of man tampering and human thinking.

Many youth pastors vainly believe that the employment of hype, entertainment and cultural relevance is the key to strategic and effective ministry. They follow the dress, piercing, and hairstyle fads of the ever fickle, rapidly changing youth that they target—thinking that renewal and transformation are happening. Yet their disciples abandon the faith in droves as soon as they enter college or go into the world to begin life as adults.

Many churches acquiesce to the current culture, allowing the opinions of secular society to dictate to them the parameters of worship. They are shaped and influenced by what their attenders want or demand, instead of solely focusing upon God, and discipling people into the peculiar nature of our foreign citizenship here on this earth.[70]

Cultural norms are allowed to impose themselves upon the Church, things such as the societal dictate that our church services cannot be longer than an hour and a half, or that the Holy Spirit should not be given the opportunity to move freely and openly in public worship services. Unfortunately, people have had negative experiences in times past with preachers who were showmen and not true men of God.

This has led to a swing of the pendulum and many leaders have ceased taking up their cross to crucify pride and have allowed popular opinion to define the Holy Spirit's movement as embarrassing.

This has led to a swing of the pendulum and many leaders have ceased taking up their cross to crucify pride and have allowed popular opinion to define the Holy Spirit's movement as embarrassing. Many flee from that opportunity because onlookers might think us drunk or hysterical, as the scoffers did in Acts,[71] yet we claim the fullness of what is written. We stand in our pulpits uttering verbal musings of what we wished we were experiencing, wondering why we do not have an open show of power in our meetings, while the vast majority of our people stumble around in a fog of selfishness, not pursuing God wholeheartedly, yet expecting God to wholeheartedly rescue them from all of their troubles.

Why do we endlessly take these things into our hands and shape them according

---

[70] 1 Peter 2:9, Titus 2:11-15

[71] Acts 2:1-41

to our experience? Why, oh why, do we take upon ourselves the pressure and responsibility to build the Church when that is what Jesus does?[72] Never were we commanded to build the Church or ministry or any other structure. All the supposed credit goes to God when we successfully attract and hold ever-growing crowds, yet we strap our staffs with veiled threats for the smooth operation and flawless execution of lights and sound. And we constantly fear the consequences of our decisions as the Church grows, hoping against hope that we will not do something to upset the balance of sustained growth.

So many pastors' lives are controlled by their workload, and they die early because they carry the weight of building the Church. This should not be. Our command is to make disciples. It is Jesus who groups them together into a church.

I am not suggesting that there should be no structure or order or sound Church government. Those are necessary and God-ordained things. What I am saying is that we should leave those things in the hands of Jesus and respond to what He does. He sometimes does things that do not make sense to us or to our experience. Sometimes, we actually work to prevent His plans without realizing it. We would never knowingly allow a thief to be our church treasurer and a betrayer to be one of our most trusted ministers, but Jesus did. That man's name was Judas.

Yes, we should all have a "spirit of excellence" because whatever we do we should do with all our heart.[73] Choose the best color scheme, have a great website, choose the right font style, and most importantly, select men and women of great character that the Lord brings to us. We must not choose them *solely* based on their personality evaluation or strengths test. That information adds to our knowledge base of the person, but ultimately we must choose someone based on the leading of the Lord.

---

[72] Matthew 16:18

[73] Colossians 3:23

When Jesus is in charge, everything He does has eternal purpose.

Our gifts, anointing, and talents are given to us in order to *respond* to what He is doing, not *determine* our ability to perform.

Our gifts, anointing, and talents are given to us in order to *respond* to what He is doing, not *determine* our ability to perform. Why do we follow our gifts and anointing rather than Jesus? Why do we take it upon ourselves to shape the altar of God? Could it be because it is embedded into our fallen nature? Could it be that we have a drive to usurp God, claiming in our hearts and on our planet His rightful position?

Indeed.

These altars have been defiled by the American dream, by marketing, merchandizing, consumerism, and materialism. They are so saturated with the wisdom of man until the true is thought false, and the false is thought true.

Our patterns have been shaped by worldly corporations and the worldly-minded men we have studied and praised. We look to secular musicians for our inspiration in worship. We have used the learning of men to shape how and what the altars have become. Then we base our justification for this upon numbers, people's response to the service, or the efficiency in which everything operates. When we do this, often in ignorance, the altars are no longer what God designed.

God's design is often unappealing in its raw form, so we take it upon ourselves to give definition to something that is Holy. We think, how ridiculous to give God the form of a calf, but is that what we are doing? If the leadership team is constantly under pressure to "improve" the service in order to hold and increase attendance, then it is doubtful that what they have is God's design.

We must realize the difference between simple expansion and true growth.

My brilliant friend, Pastor Bob Moody, said: the difference between expansion and growth can be determined by whether the congregation can heal itself or not after injury happens. A balloon expands rapidly and when it pops it can't recover. A tree grows slowly, and if a branch is cut or breaks off, it heals and continues to grow.

When Moses was drawn to the marvel of the bush that burned yet was not consumed, God called him close and then stopped him: "Do not come any closer," God said. "Take off your sandals, for the place where you are standing is holy ground" (Exodus 3:5).

Why was it necessary for Moses to remove his sandals? Why would God call him close, and then stop him short?

Who made the dirt of the ground that had been sanctified by the presence of God? God had.

Who made the feet in the sandals that were walking toward the presence of God Almighty? God did.

Who made the sandals? Some man or woman had made the sandals.

God does not want manmade things between Him and us. Man ideas, man intellect, man learning, and man arrogance—these filters defile and contaminate whatever they touch. God is holy and He is saying not to defile His stuff!

We can approach, but only if we are surrendered to Him and not be those who demand our own way. We must take off our sandals before we approach Him.

Consider the following verses from the New Testament:

"Now this is our boast: Our conscience testifies that we have conducted ourselves in the world, and especially in our relations with you, in the holiness and sincerity that are from God. We have done so not according to worldly wisdom but according to God's grace."[74]

"My message and my preaching were not with wise and persuasive words, but with a demonstration of the Spirit's power, so that your faith might not rest on men's wisdom, but on God's power."[75]

"We have not received the spirit of the world but the Spirit who is from God, that we may understand what God has freely given us. This is what we speak, not in words taught us by human wisdom but in words taught by the Spirit, expressing spiritual truths in spiritual words. The man without the Spirit does not accept the things that come from the Spirit of God, for they are foolishness to him, and he cannot understand them, because they are spiritually discerned."[76]

"But God chose the foolish things of the world to shame the wise; God chose the weak things of the world to shame the strong. He chose the lowly things of this world and the despised things—and the things that are not—to nullify the things that are, so that no one may boast before him."[77]

"For the kingdom of God is not a matter of talk but of power."[78]

Many people ask me why I think the church in the United States is essentially powerless and rarely sees miracles. I believe that 1 Corinthians 1:17 explains it succinctly: "For Christ did not send me to baptize, but to preach the gospel—not with words of human wisdom, lest the cross of Christ be emptied of its power."

---

[74] 2 Corinthians 1:12

[75] 1 Corinthians 2:4-5

[76] 1 Corinthians 2:12-14

[77] 1 Corinthians 1:27-29

[78] 1 Corinthians 4:20

It is the preaching of the Gospel mixed with words of human wisdom that empties the Cross of its power. We are God's building, made up of living stones, so we must stop shaping people with human philosophy and sterile doctrines that strip the Cross of its power. We must add demonstration to our teaching and lay open our lives so that others will see *and* hear.[79] To believe that the power of the Cross is only for "salvation" is such a sad human limitation. The Cross, because of the meaning of the awesome sacrifice of the Lord Jesus, is the absolute defining event of history. There the enemy was defeated and we who follow Jesus were given the rights and abilities that come along with being children of the living King of kings.

Jesus is alive! Accept Him, die daily, and He will live in YOU!

> We are God's building, made up of living stones, so we must stop shaping people with human philosophy and sterile doctrines that strip the Cross of its power.

[79] Matthew 11:4

1 9

Raising the Dead

Jesus' creative power knows no boundaries, which is an undisputed fact in the heart of all who believe. Where the problem arises is in what we believe regarding God's intention and plan to use His power to work miracles among us today.

By now in reading this book, you know that I am convinced that Jesus can and still does work miracles regularly and inseparably with the spreading of the Gospel. I believe that the definitive evidence to assist the fruitful propagation of the Gospel, no matter what country, culture, religion, or people, is an open show of the power of God. His presence and power cannot be replaced by any contrivance or action of man.

The mountains where we minister are quite steep and it rains constantly. In 2006 I measured the annual rainfall at over two hundred inches! There are deep canyons with rivers and streams in the bottom, so in a monsoon these watercourses can be extremely dangerous to cross.

One of my coworkers once encountered a pastor from another mission effort who had been visiting a small family in a remote village. There was no road to this village, and the only way to reach it was to cross a deep canyon. This pastor had been struggling to be faithful to this newly saved family, and he was finding it impossible in some cases to make his scheduled visits to them. Their hut was at the top of their village, which was about a two thousand-foot vertical climb above the base of this knife-edged mountain range. Getting there regularly was wearing him out, so he asked us if we would take over these visits, and we gladly accepted.

We began to visit this man. His name is Cristobal, his wife's name is Cristina, and their two-year-old adopted daughter is Lupita. We went week after week, making the beautiful hike to their hut. We did our best to speak life from the Bible to Cristobal and his family. He smiled a lot but said little. Cristina was full of vigor for Jesus, because she had been healed of breast cancer when she was saved. Her husband was more reserved—until December 31, 2008, when something extraordinary happened. The next time we were at their house, this couple calmly related the amazing story of what Jesus had done for them.

Little Lupita had fallen ill with bronchitis, and after several days her condition had grown steadily worse. On December 30 her parents put her to bed and then laid down themselves, worried because of the little girl's condition.

At 5:30 a.m. on December 31 Cristina woke up to check on Lupita who was in her little homemade crib, lovingly fashioned from carved sticks, and found her cold and stiff. She had died in the night and rigor mortis had set in. Cristina woke up Cristobal, and they began to pray that their daughter would be brought back to life! They prayed for about two hours, but when she failed to revive, they decided to take the body in to the authorities to execute a death certificate.

Before leaving, Cristobal went to bathe, all the while continuing to pray. Cristina, who was preparing the things they needed to take to the authorities, also continued to pray. While they both were calling out to God, Lupita stood up and asked for a piece of candy! Her mom and dad came running, and they gave her that piece of candy! The little girl then climbed out of her crib and began to run and play in the house. What joy! What amazing power! Jesus had raised Lupita from the dead!

Indeed, He is the same yesterday, today, and forever.[80]

The parents decided to take their daughter to the doctor anyway to verify that she was okay. The doctor examined Lupita and said that there was nothing wrong and that her bronchitis was gone. When Lupita had died, the sickness that had killed her died also!

What do you make of this? Do you believe that a miracle like this can happen today? If you don't, why not?[81]

———————

Sometime later we had a campaign where we had about three hundred people gathered. I asked Cristobal to testify about what God had done for his daughter. He stood awkwardly, stared at the ground, and talked for less than two minutes. He had few words and shared few of the details of this miracle.

Cristina was unsatisfied with her husband's testimony, so she asked if she could share, too. She held Lupita as she explained in detail what Jesus had done: He had given them back Lupita after she had been dead for several hours.

As time passed I began noticing a change in Cristobal's life. He began to show more desire to accompany us from place to place, even walking for hours to get to where our truck would pass by so he could go to church with us, and many times his wife and daughter were with him. I could see that Jesus was working in his heart, but he still had very little to say when I asked him to share in a meeting.

---

[80] Hebrews 13:8

[81] Acts 26:8

Then the Lord began crafting a great unity among our people, which was quite an unusual occurrence. People from different locales in the area started showing up at church services, wanting to worship together. A tremendous excitement and hunger for God arose in the people. We had worked in the area for six years and something new was happening!

One night I hauled sixty-five people in the back of a big truck we used for that purpose to a service in a village. We packed them into a hut with no room to spare. That night as I was praying during worship, the Lord said to me, "Tell the people that I am going to pour out My Spirit and send My presence to them tonight. I want you to change the schedule for the next ten days and hold services in the ten main villages. (These ten anchor villages were situated among many other villages in a broad area where we had strong work going.) I am going to pour out My presence in every place! Tell them this plan now. Go and tell all the people what is happening and gather them together for every service. Go and sow the fire I am sending!"

I responded to the Lord by telling Him that this is what we had been praying for, but what if what I had just "heard" was only wishful thinking on my part? To try to bring together two hundred people—to meet in someone's house with less than twenty-four hours' notice—had the potential of destroying the work we'd been doing.

The people we work with are so concerned about being good hosts. This plan essentially meant that we were going to be on the move for ten days, each night in a different place. Normally, when we plan a campaign, it takes the hosts two to three days to prepare the food. There would be some advance notice for those places we would be going to in a few days, but what about the meeting tomorrow? And how could I even find everybody spread across multiple villages on short notice to tell them of the meetings? There was no quick and easy way to do this. None of them had phones. Some did not even have electricity.

Tomorrow they would be scattered out, working their fields in places that I did not even know about. How could I contact them? There would be no time to prepare food for the service tomorrow, and the offense of such failed hospitality in this culture would be hard to overcome—if God was not in this plan.

All the cultural training I'd received over the past eleven years, frankly, made this venture seem kind of crazy. Weren't we going to put way too much pressure on these poor people? If I told everyone what God had promised and then nothing different happened in the services, I would be seen as a liar and the momentum for winning souls to Christ would die.

At least that's how I was seeing this from a human perspective.

So before things got "out of control," like a dumb person, I decided to argue with God, fearing that I might not have heard His voice correctly.

The Lord answered me, and in "clarifying" things, only made my wobbling faith worse: He said, "If there is no risk, then it certainly is not Me."

I asked Him, "Why does the risk need to be so high?" This time He didn't answer! That usually means the conversation is over and, spiritually speaking, it's time to fish or cut bait.

So I had to swallow my pride, plunge into faith, and begin to talk about what the Lord was going to do and the plans for the coming days. And the Lord whispered to me as I began, "I have given them one heart and one mind. I have given them a hunger for Me. Are you going to be the one who keeps the door closed to them? They will follow you. Lead them to My presence. I have seen to it that you have never lied to them. They will believe you."

So with a good dose of fear and trembling, I told them that God was going to pour out His Spirit upon them that night, and I explained that we were going to have services in our main churches over the next ten nights.

Then we began to worship God. There was such expectation and hunger as the people truly worshiped our King with their whole heart. I had not seen them move toward God like this before. We worshiped and worshiped, forgetting the time and place. The songs they sing are simple, and the musicians are not practiced. The music, if it were recorded and put on a CD, would not sell to very many people. But the worship comes out of their hearts! Some of them cannot keep rhythm when they clap, and not many can sing well, but when the Spirit of God is upon them, they respond with their whole being. There have been open-eyed visions and encounters of various kinds. A few times, God has come so suddenly upon a place that the building or ground was shaken. Manifestations of Heaven's dimension have broken in on our reality on numerous occasions. God responds to those who pursue Him with a whole heart.

At some point in the middle of the worship, I waded into the crowd and began praying for them. The power of God began to move and His presence was overwhelming! The fire of God seized people as they responded by abandoning themselves to Him. Many, because of the weight of God's presence, could not stay on their feet and crumpled to the floor. Others had visions. Tino, our main national leader, put his hands up and felt fire burning just above his head. All the little kids present broke out dancing. Everyone seemed caught up in something that they had never experienced and were on fire with a drive to spread the message of the Gospel.

The people could not wait for tomorrow! This experience was not one they had participated in, observed on TV, or read about in a book or on the Internet. They don't have access to those things to have had their emotions conditioned to some kind of emotional response, as some have suggested to me as I have shared this story. This work was pure and new.

I don't believe in "coaching" people to generate "experiences." I have been pushed down at altars by charlatans who were little more than snake-oil salesmen, who use the "charismatic experience" to build their own private kingdom. They rely on emotions and coaching to work people up, conditioning them into particular manifestations. I detest any prostitution of the presence of God.

That's not what was happening here! When God truly comes, no one remains the same. God had sent His Spirit and baptized our people with fire! His presence had broken forth out of their response to Him.

———

We started early the next day to find and inform the rest of our believers about what was happening. Every place we went the men were all somehow either at home or close by their house. We found every person! This could only happen if God were doing something. We went to twenty villages that day, looking for many people, and found every person!

Everyone we talked to was feeling hunger for God. They were all extremely excited, and that night we hauled 110 people to the meeting site. Once again, the presence of God broke out among us in an even greater way. Somehow, in every service we went to, all the cultural benchmarks were met without a hitch. Everybody served food, and all the logistics were flawlessly executed! Jesus wove all of the details together and everything worked perfectly. My fears were unrealized!

Every day we followed the plan God had given me. Each night, in every place, the increased presence broke out among us. Miracles were popping! One hundred twenty people got saved during the course of those services and in the following days. Up until then, we had been seeing about twenty to thirty conversions per month. Suddenly, as a result of the outbreak of the fire of God, there was a fourfold jump in the salvation of souls.

After this series of services we phased back to our normal schedule. We continued to have church every day in a different village, twenty-eight days per month. God's presence continued to burn among us and our harvest of souls increased. Our native pastors were ignited to work for the Kingdom of God.

As a result of the energy of God coming on our people, Cristobal suddenly was thrust out of his stoic, speechless life. He began to share from the Scriptures when we had a service at his house. He also began to go out on his own and lead people to Jesus. Cristobal has never been silenced since.

As he began to seek souls for Jesus, he started to see dramatic miracles. One day he hiked over to a village to visit with another of our national pastors. The other pastor was usually the one who took the lead on such a visit and was responsible for encouraging him to work for Jesus.

When Cristobal arrived, however, the other pastor was not there. The people in the village were very disturbed about something and asked impatiently if Cristobal knew where the other pastor was. He responded that he didn't but said, "I'm here." He was told there was an urgent problem in the next village. A little boy had died about two hours earlier, and villagers had come to get the pastor and believers to pray over the boy.

So Cristobal told them that he would come. He cancelled the scheduled service and he and the others began the fifteen-minute walk to the other village. And Cristobal, whose own daughter had been raised from the dead, began to pray, saying to God, "Lord, I have doubt. I can't do this!"

He heard the Lord respond, "It's okay, son; who is it you are asking for help?" He said, "You, Lord. I am asking You for help." God said to him, "That's right, you are asking Me for help. And I don't have any doubt!"

> "That's right, you are asking Me for help. And I don't have any doubt!"

Cristobal told me later that this gave him great peace and joy. Of course! God does not have any doubt! So he continued to pray as they finished walking to the house where the little boy lay.

Upon arriving he and the other believers with him began to pray, calling out to God for an hour. They prayed fervently, so earnestly until they found themselves shouting out to God to have mercy and put life back in that boy. Then the little boy sat up! Everyone in the house was filled with awe and joy. Then they shouted praises to God for another hour!

Since we arrived at this new mission field in 2003, many people have died, but seven of them were prayed for and came back to life and are alive to this day—healed from what had killed them.

What marvelous things we can see if we genuinely introduce people to Jesus! What possible advantage could we gain by not believing He is still the same today? He is who He says He is in His book.

Why not just believe Him?

2 0

What Is Normal to God?

You remember the story of Mario, the rancher who gave his life to Jesus—then was the host for the miraculous meal of chicken and rice (see Chapter 13)?

As you might expect there are more chapters to Mario's story.

Most of those in Mario's extended family were not happy at all about his conversion and became extremely cold to him and his wife. Even though he was a grown man in his forties with a family, they wanted to rein him in and make him conform to their religious ideals. His mother would have liked to disinherit him, and his younger brother, who was about my age, turned caustic and bitter. The rancher's two sisters listened to what he told them of his new faith and were interested.

But it was painfully obvious that Jesus had divided Mario's family, and some family members even became his enemies because he no longer worshiped their idols.

Mario and his wife read where Jesus said He would be a divider of even close family members.[82] When they read this they were encouraged because they saw that what the Bible said was really true.

---

[82] Luke 12:51

Mario's younger brother openly showed his hate for my family and me. If he met us on the road, in spite of our friendly waves, he would turn his head away so that he would not have to look at us. If we encountered him in Mario's store, he would turn his back and walk out as soon as we entered. We made it a point always to greet him with a smile, but he never responded except with venom in his eyes, if he met our gaze at all. We continued to pray earnestly for him.

One day all the rancher's brothers were down on their ranch, rounding up cattle, herding them into corrals in preparation for a cattle sale. Cattle and men were everywhere, dust rising in thick clouds from all the activity. As the men were forcing the cattle to enter a corral, a large cow with long horns decided to break ranks with the herd. The brother who disliked us so much ran to cut the cow off. Both the cow and the man were running along the outside of the corral, but on different sides, this being a square catch pen.

Because of the pen's high boards the cow and the brother could not see each other. They converged at a corner at the same time, colliding in full stride. The cow weighed over one thousand pounds, the man about one hundred and eighty, so it was a calamity for the younger brother, who was thrown through the air, landing in a heap on the ground, lifeless. The collision had killed him.

Mario's young sons, who had gotten saved around the time that their parents did, ran to help their uncle, their dad getting there shortly after the accident. All of them began to pray earnestly, calling out to God, whom the dead man hated, for mercy. The sons prayed fervently while their dad administered CPR in an effort to revive his brother, who showed no vital signs. The prayer and CPR continued for another fifteen minutes but nothing changed. The injured man showed no sign of life.

Without God's intervention, there was no hope. Something supernatural needed to occur.

What is *normal* to God? What is His definition of *normal* for us? What does He expect His effect to be in us, on us, and around us? Are there really any limits in Him? Yet we live as if there are. We think as if there are. We are guided by this supposition.

God says *believe*. Be like a child and let flow *possibility*, inspired into erupting reality by our proximity to Him. It is all about Him. He is our King—the King of kings. We are destined to do extraordinary things for the glory of our King.

The difference between what is normal to us and what is normal to God becomes clear in our relationship with Him. We don't often sit long enough in His presence to learn to hear Him clearly. So we miss out.

I have so often pondered why it is that we have defined *normal* as it relates to God's involvement with us, to mean merely the dull and powerless boundaries of human ability. Jesus is alive and His intention is to clearly communicate with us in a way that is amazing—if we value above all else our relationship with Him. So many do not experience the fact that He can speak clearly and in great detail on a daily basis if we seek Him with intentional but reckless abandon.

God speaks to us through a plethora of avenues: His Word, circumstances, other people, and directly by the Holy Spirit. However, so often we fail to value focused time with Him, just the two of us in conversation. So we don't hear what He is saying directly and specifically to us. It does take time to build such an intimate relationship with Him, to learn to clearly identify His voice. God has His reasons for having a "still, small voice."

By comparison, reading His Word is a relatively easy discipline. I believe the Holy Scripture is meant to establish the outer boundaries of our relationship with God, across which we should not wander. His

Voice certainly is found in Scripture, but so many people use the intellectual understanding of Scripture, knowing *about* Him, as a replacement for actually *knowing* Him.

Prayer is the means that connects us most intimately with God and it carries various forms. Worship is prayer's highest form. Intercession is prayer's work. Petition is only one form of communicating with Him but, sadly, to present God with endless petitions is so often the only prayer engagement most people have, if they pray at all. To listen, though, that is a difficult treasure to discover.

If you have never heard His voice, let this inspire you to begin your seeking in earnest. If you have heard His voice in the past, but feel stagnant, let this inspire you to rouse yourself out of your stupor and start seeking with your whole heart. If you are running strong, run deeper!

Prayer is not the utterance of a special vocabulary, but rather what comes directly from your heart in raw form. This is not something that can be explained in a step-by-step format. It is something only understood as it is practiced. As you begin to encounter God, hunger for God is born. Hunger fuels ever increasing grasping to *know* Him, and that is why God shrouds Himself in mystery, so we will seek Him out. The deeper the mystery grows, the harder we seek. And once we have tasted…

Let Jesus teach you how to hear Him.[83]

The only thing that Jesus' disciples asked Him to teach them was to teach them *to* pray.[84] This is not to be confused with the teaching of *how* to pray. The *how* is simple—talk with God with your whole heart. It is the *doing* of prayer that is so hard to maintain. Just do it. Just get with God, every day, and start talking with Him, seeking to find Him with all of your heart. If you do this, everything will change.

---

[83] Matthew 7:7-8

[84] Luke 11:1

Somewhere, in the vastness of the close confines of our own limitations, God will be found speaking. See to it that you are listening in the deep silence, for He will be met by you there, eagerly awaiting your visit so that you can become the message, His message.

After persisting with CPR on his brother for a good while—perhaps twenty minutes, Mario gave up. The workers pulled a pickup truck near and loaded the younger brother's dead body into the back. His nephews climbed in beside their dead uncle but did not stop praying. As Mario was walking from the back of the truck to the cab, the dead man woke up and spoke, asking what had happened! Everyone, except for the brother who had come back from the dead, was amazed and began praising God!

> See to it that you are listening in the deep silence, for He will be met by you there, eagerly awaiting your visit so that you can become the message, His message.

Later, after a doctor had examined the man, it turned out that he had no discoverable injuries. God had heard the prayers, intervened, and raised the uncle from the dead, even though he had intense disdain for God, his brother, and those who had shared the love of God with him.

I did not learn of this incident until later that afternoon. We were having a service in a village that night, so at the meeting I asked everyone to pray for this man that God had shown mercy to. As he returned from the hospital, having been given a clean bill of health, Mario told his brother how I had asked everybody to pray for his complete healing that night. Since then the brother will greet me if we happen to meet. He is less hostile toward the Gospel, but he still persists in his unbelief, occasionally lapsing back into his former poisoned attitude with his brother.

The nature of any man's rebellion is such that even getting run over by a thousand pound cow, dying, being raised from the dead, and receiving the good will of those you hate with a vengeance is not enough to get your attention!

———

So often, as we ponder the supernatural—that which is normal to God—we think that such an encounter will either "dehumanize" us or transform us into super-disciples. It does neither. We believe that if God were to do dramatic things, undeniable things, then all who see and hear them would believe. Only some believe, others remain in their unbelief and rebellion.

Supernatural encounters make a plain statement that there is something powerful and inexplicable beyond ourselves. After the encounter, though, we are still left with the human function of choosing to follow or not. Miracles do not make instant disciples, nor do they ensure that we will walk in complete obedience to God. Even Jesus, after working many miracles, found Himself virtually abandoned at the cross. After He rose from the dead and went to the right hand of the Father, the believers were a group of only about one hundred and twenty.[85] So many people had been healed of their sicknesses while He was ministering on earth. Did they stay true to Him? Just take the one miracle when more than five thousand people ate the multiplied food, where were they?

---

[85] Acts 1:15

After a miracle occurs we still have a nature that needs transforming and God has seen to it that the transforming of that nature requires constant relationship, because that is what He desires most from us.

Roberto, who had been healed of throat cancer in such a dramatic and undeniable fashion, decided after three years of regularly hearing the gospel that he would not give up his idols and he returned to his family's demonic traditions. He turned his back on Jesus, the One who had saved his life.

In the end, what God is really looking for is that we choose Him because He IS, not because we have demanded some kind of empirical proof.[86] We must not put any conditions upon God.

---

[86] John 20:29, Matthew 12:38-39

21

Suffering

Suffering produces one of two things in us:
Bitterness or Brokenness
Brokenness produces one of two things in us:
Humility or Self-pity
Humility, once gained, must be fought for to keep.

The things we suffer teach us obedience. And perseverance.[87]

So much bad doctrine has been propagated concerning suffering, either for or against it. As Americans our preoccupation with materialistic prosperity, as well as the fact that we live in the world's only remaining superpower, saturates our subconscious and hinders our ability to truly understand what the Bible says. It's the filter that colors our worldview.

Of course, no one in his right mind wants to suffer. However, if we follow Jesus, He will lead us into many deserted and dry places, deserts where it may be painful but also impossible not to recognize His hand.

Suffering will perfect us—if we are submitted to Jesus. If not, then we will wander in aimless circles, still subject to intense problems but

---

[87] James 1:1-4

never able to advance beyond the madness and bitterness caused by the inevitable disappointment and pain of life on earth. To be pragmatic, on our pathway of life's problems, we might just as well go ahead and get the eternal benefit out of walking faithfully! We will if we follow Jesus.

When Jesus said, "It is finished," this was not Jesus in crisis management; it was a rebirth of His original intention.

All suffering and struggle stop as we pass from this life on earth into eternity with Jesus.[88] The death of Jesus purchased our eternal freedom from sin and sin's effect upon us. This gives us the opportunity to walk with God for eternity as it was originally intended.

We must follow and obey Jesus no matter what comes. We cannot put conditions upon our walking down the road that Jesus has chosen for us. It takes patient endurance to walk with God. In fact, without endurance no one will see God.[89] Without Him we can do nothing, and He is most persistent that we learn that.[90] We must remain steadfast in our decision to walk with God and receive tenacity in our faith, because patient endurance comes from Jesus.[91] It is only when there is a reason for faith that we understand the application for faith.

The reason that we have faith as a gift is so that we can draw near to God and see God overcome impossible situations in our lives. The gift of healing exists because there is sickness. Self-control is one of the fruits of the Spirit because there is something inside of us that needs controlling. Suffering and problems are the opportunities given to us so that obedience has a platform from which to operate and faith can "work." Jesus Himself learned from the things that He suffered.[92]

---

[88] Revelation 21:4

[89] Hebrews 10:32-36, 2 Corinthians 6:3-10, James 1:12, Romans 2:7

[90] John 15:5, Isaiah 26:12

[91] 2 Thessalonians 3:5

[92] Hebrews 5:8

We are not beat down. We are not barely hanging on. We are astounded by great joy, and at times, great sorrow. We know some of the fellowship of the sufferings of Christ. We have submitted to Him, and that submission has put us in the right place at the right time to see dramatic miracles. How could we be unaffected when the Creator intervenes in our dimension and works something impossible?

But suffering is suffering. It hurts and it often defies our ability to find reason for it. It is up to *us* how we respond to suffering. The struggle does not have the power to *force* us to sour and become bitter. If we have the Spirit of God dwelling within us, nothing can *make* us bitter. If bitterness takes root in us, it is because *we* became bitter. Nothing forced that bitterness upon us. Jesus works every circumstance to our benefit if we are surrendered to Him.[93] As Audrey has said for years, "It's a *choice* to rejoice."[94]

In 2004 we were fighting hard to open the Gospel in the area God had sent us to. In some months I preached seventy times. We were seeing dramatic results in new villages opened, miracles, and souls won to Christ, but in the middle of this exciting ministry "success," our two daughters, Hannah and Aspen, along with our son, Jacob, came down with some type of sickness. Their symptoms were chest pain, achiness, headache, stomach pain, sore throat, a bit of diarrhea, lethargy, and weakness. The girls recovered after a month, but Jacob did not. His symptoms worsened and he became very weak.

As I've already discussed, so often during our work in Mexico the health of our kids has been attacked. The spiritual and mental toughness

---

[93] Romans 8:28

[94] Philippians 4:4-7

required from these times has been perhaps the most difficult challenge of this life of faith we live.

When serious health issues arise in our kids, Audrey, or me we do not automatically go to the doctor. We are not opposed to doctors and have often received help from professionals in the medical community, including Audrey's father who is a pediatrician. However, when we need healing in our physical body, we do our best via our faith to let Jesus—the ultimate Physician and Healer—respond first.

In this situation with Jacob, we waited, prayed, and fasted. We also asked many other people to pray with us. We stood for ten weeks, but Jacob's health continued to deteriorate, and we still did not know exactly what was wrong with him.

During this time period I was leaving the house early most days, responding to the marked increase of new villages and converts. Many days I was out until late at night and returned home exhausted—both by the work and the ever increasing emotional load of Jacob's condition.

Sometimes I would drag myself into Jacob's room and find Audrey holding him in bed, tears running down her face as she prayed, "God, please don't let him die. Help him breathe." I would pray for him, too, then bring Audrey to our room and hold her as she cried, both of us wondering what the outcome would be.

Sometimes I would lie in our bed and stare at the ceiling, spiritually numb from the incongruence of our situation. On one hand we were experiencing great Gospel advances on a daily basis with new territory opening, new people coming to Christ, and awesome miracles. Yet in spite of fervent prayer from people living in multiple countries, our son was wasting away, unable to do much more than lie in the bed or roll around our house in an office chair with wheels.

A thousand nightmares cannot compare to watching your child waste away when you can do nothing about it. I did not understand why we were seeing dramatic healings in the village work we were doing, yet I could not see my son healed...

And this was not the first time we had faced a life-threatening affliction in our children.

In August 2004, the month before Jacob got sick, I took him and two visitors, Steve and Jace Hassoldt, to a village about a forty-five minute drive from our house for a service. As we were sitting in the house of Chucho, one of our pastors, he told me about a neighbor woman named Josefina who was very sick. He asked if we could go and try to lead her to Jesus and then pray for her. Of course we could, so we got up and walked through the woods to Josefina's house.

We entered her dim and dirty hut but only saw the woman's husband. We began to talk with him about Jesus but he was not very interested, saying that he wanted nothing to do with the Gospel but he did want his wife healed!

As we conversed I wondered where Josefina was and then, from behind a sheet of colorful plastic that made a room partition in their small house, I heard her voice. She was mostly hidden behind this plastic wall, with her hands clasped in front of her. Through the plastic sheet we began to share the Gospel with Josefina, and she was receptive to the message of the love of God and received Jesus!

After Josefina was born again, I asked her and her husband what her sickness was. As is very common with the mountain people, the answers were vague. I also kept inching my way closer to the plastic barrier so that I might possibly get a glimpse and see what her problem was.

When I finally did get a good look, my heart went out to her. Josefina's hands and face were covered in the white patches of a leper. That is why she was hiding, because of her shunned condition.

I gently asked Josefina if in fact she had leprosy, and she confirmed that this was true. We invited her to come out from behind the screen and asked if we could lay hands on her and call out to God for her cleansing. She let us. Before we left I explained to Josefina that it was imperative that she seek God and that she needed to come to Chucho's house when we came to have church so that she could hear the Word of God. We were holding a church service there once a week and invited her to join us that night.

The four of us walked back to Chucho's house where we had church. We sat on narrow boards that lined a room that measured about 7' x 14'. After eating a meal with the people who had come, we began the service with some praise music. As we sang and clapped, I noticed in the interior of the adjoining room where the cooking fire was that Josefina was standing against the far wall in the dimmest shadows next to the door, next to the fire that still had embers glowing.

After that evening, every time we were there for church, Josefina, still obviously suffering with leprosy, would wait until it was dark and we had started the service, then slip in the back door.

This pattern continued for many weeks. The woman would only come out of the cooking room to get prayer at the very end of the service, and then quickly she would disappear out the back and into the dark jungle beyond.

My heart was heavy for her. I can still see her eyes, open wide in the darkness of the cooking room, listening but afraid to come three feet into the room with other people. Josefina's countenance was crestfallen, yet she was hearing the message of hope and the application of that transforming message through the testimonies shared at those services.

One day in October, two months after Josefina gave her heart to Jesus, Audrey, our friends Mark and Christie Marble, and I were sitting in the main room of the house where we had church when Josefina walked in through the front door—in the daylight—and came directly to me and said, "I am healed and I can see!" Her face and hands had new skin! Josefina had been cleansed. I had no idea until she told me that day that she had been having trouble with her eyes as well. I now learned that she'd been almost totally blind, and when Jesus took her leprosy, He also healed her eyes! What an incredible miracle!

However, the joy of seeing Jesus work such an awesome miracle for Josefina was clouded because during the same time period, our own son Jacob was wasting away at home. He had become ill after this lady had been saved, and yet he still was getting worse. Many of our supporters and supporting churches communicated with us that they were praying for Jacob. This could number in the thousands! Yet Josefina, with leprosy and blindness, was fully healed!

———

I was in turmoil. On one hand, because of the power of God we were seeing in the work we were doing, I felt like I could charge the gates of hell! On the other hand, I felt like we were losing our son. Jacob was slipping away, and we could not stop the slide. It reminded me acutely of what had happened with my sister. Audrey was in the same turmoil. We proclaimed the healing power of Jesus and we didn't want to give up. We wanted to see a miracle. As we made the difficult decision to go to the doctor she told me she only wanted to take him if God would still get the glory. After ten weeks of prayer, fasting, doing blood work at the local clinic, and treating him for parasites, we decided to try to find a competent doctor in Mexico and try to learn what was wrong with Jacob.

We found a competent doctor four hours away and took him there. After doing blood work, the Mexican physician diagnosed him with salmonella typhi, also known as typhoid fever. The doctor could not believe that he had been sick for ten weeks. He was very concerned and demanded that we put Jacob in the hospital. This sickness was the number one killer of children in Mexico. It is so potent that it often kills a child in only two to three weeks. That's why the doctor was so concerned. He said the only reason Jacob was alive was that our God had placed a star on his forehead. He gave God the glory!!!

We appreciated his concern but balked at his suggestion because most hospitals in Mexico were notoriously bad, and there was no way we were going to turn Jacob over to an institution where he might die. I told the doctor we were not taking him to the hospital. The doctor got mad at me and said, "Well, I am not responsible for what happens to your son. He is very sick. He could die any day."

I answered that he was never responsible for my son: "God is my son's shield," I told him. I also said that we would do whatever he suggested, take whatever medicines he prescribed, but that we would do so at our home where we could take care of him.

The doctor prescribed some extremely potent medicine for Jacob, and we began this treatment, now having the knowledge of what we were facing. We followed the doctor's instructions and returned for another appointment and found that the treatment was working. By the third visit the doctor pronounced him cured of this sickness. The medicine that he was on, which penetrated even to his bone marrow, weakened him so badly that it took Jacob six months to recover from the medication.

———

Then in 2005 our youngest son, David, began to feel sickly. It was nothing we could identify—he just didn't feel well. He was weak and lethargic. This was so abnormal for him, because he was, and is, extremely active and creative, always moving about inventing and innovating new things. Now this sickness was like a phantom with lukewarm fingers that had our son by the throat, slowly choking the life from him, bleeding his energy until all he could do was lie in bed day after day, looking hollow, rarely leaving his room.

Audrey and I were assaulted with weariness. David could not keep up with his schoolwork and got further and further behind. Medical assessments revealed nothing of consequence. Here we were with yet another inexplicable sickness slowly draining away the life of one of our children.

There were periods of time where we thought he'd been healed and would rally from his weakness. Then David would try something, resume some activity, and would end up back in bed again. It seemed that every time we would rejoice at seeming improvement, the very rejoicing would push him back down into the same old pit. This was so much like what had happened with Hannah years earlier.

In 2010, on his fourteenth birthday, he started to feel better! What a gift to all of us. He has had good days and bad days since then. At this point, complete healing has eluded us as he still struggles with feeling good. We have done tests and prayed and done treatments. We don't have an answer, yet during those tough years we saw the Kingdom of God take root where it had never before germinated.

What is my point with telling you all of this?

Depending on what you believe about healing, you may judge us for waiting so long to take Jacob to the doctor, or you may judge us for taking him to the doctor and using medicine. We did all that we could, and responded to the situation as best we knew how. I realize that our experience does not fit with some faith healing doctrine. I also realize that how we responded initially does not make sense to people who don't believe in healing. I do not see what happened as "either - or." It is what it is.

All I know, is that *nothing*—not life, nor death, not angels, nor demons, not trials, nor suffering—can separate us from the love of Christ. God's love is not only aimed at us for ourselves, it is also aimed aggressively at others through us. That means that God may, because of His love for *others*, send us, dead to ourselves, to reach them with His love. If we believe that struggle, or sickness, or death should *automatically* call us off the mission that He has sent us on, we live in conflict with His stated purpose.

Please read and carefully consider Romans 8:28-39:

> *And we know that in all things God works for the good of those who love him, who have been called according to his purpose. For those God foreknew he also predestined to be conformed to the likeness of his Son, that he might be the firstborn among many brothers. And those he predestined, he also called; those he called, he also justified; those he justified, he also glorified.*

> *What, then, shall we say in response to this? If God is for us, who can be against us? He who did not spare his own Son, but gave him up for us all—how will he not also, along with him, graciously give*

> God may, because of His love for *others*, send us, dead to ourselves, to reach them with His love. If we believe that struggle, or sickness, or death should *automatically* call us off the mission that He has sent us on, we live in conflict with His stated purpose.

us all things? Who will bring any charge against those whom God has chosen? It is God who justifies. Who is he that condemns? Christ Jesus, who died—more than that, who was raised to life—is at the right hand of God and is also interceding for us. Who shall separate us from the love of Christ? Shall trouble or hardship or persecution or famine or nakedness or danger or sword? As it is written:

"For your sake we face death all day long;
we are considered as sheep to be slaughtered."

No, in all these things we are more than conquerors through him who loved us. For I am convinced that neither death nor life, neither angels nor demons, neither the present nor the future, nor any powers, neither height nor depth, nor anything else in all creation, will be able to separate us from the love of God that is in Christ Jesus our Lord (Emphasis added).

Being His ambassadors means that we no longer live for ourselves. We live in Him and are extensions of His love to others as we lay down our own lives and families so that the ministry of reconciliation can be carried out on this earth.

Christ's love is the thing that compels us in the ministry of reconciliation He has given us. We should allow nothing to separate us from that "love-compelling" we have received from Him. Only Jesus can say what He wants. Nothing has the power, and we don't have the right, to change our orders. Not miracles, not the death of a loved one, not sickness, not health, not success, and not failure. To assume that any circumstance can dictate a change is sin.

Now take the time to ponder 2 Corinthians 5:11-21:

Since, then, we know what it is to fear the Lord, we try to persuade men. What we are is plain to God, and I hope it is also plain to your conscience. We are not trying to commend ourselves to you again, but are giving you an opportunity to take pride in us, so that *you can answer those who take pride in what is seen rather than in what is in the heart. If we are out of our mind, it is for the sake of God; if we are in our right mind, it is for you.* <u>*For Christ's love compels us*</u> (Emphasis added), *because we are convinced that one died for all, and therefore all died. And he died for all, that those who live should no longer live for themselves but for him who died for them and was raised again.*

So from now on we regard no one from a worldly point of view. Though we once regarded Christ in this way, we do so no longer. Therefore, if anyone is in Christ, he is a new creation; the old has gone, the new has come! All this is from God, who reconciled us to himself through Christ and gave us the ministry of reconciliation: that God was reconciling the world to himself in Christ, not counting men's sins against them. And he has committed to us the message of reconciliation. We are therefore Christ's ambassadors, as though God were making his appeal through us. We implore you on Christ's behalf: Be reconciled to God. God made him who had no sin to be sin for us, so that in him we might become the righteousness of God.

It's not just God's love *toward* us. It is God's love *in* us *to* **others**. The love of God that we have in us is for others, as well as for ourselves.

We must set our faces like flint on Jesus and not waver to the right or the left, no matter the price that He asks of us. This is the cost that we are to count.[95]

If the Lord had told us to go back to the States and get treatment for our kids, we would have, gladly. But He didn't, so we didn't.

We are ambassadors of a theocracy. There is no vote. Our only choices are either to submit and obey or to do what we want to do, often deceived by the circumstances we find ourselves in.

---

[95] Luke 14:26-30 *v28

I have no answer, though, for why our children have suffered with their health. It has been our most difficult valley to walk through. Our daughter, Aspen, has had abdominal pain every day since she was four years old, but her cheerful attitude and spirit are an inspiration to us all. After many tests and much searching, we have never found out what is causing her problem. We have spent thousands of hours in prayer for her, fasted days on end, yet there is no relief for her. As she endures her situation with godly patience, Audrey and I watch her with gripping sadness. Yet, the perfecting by the Lord that Aspen is walking in is amazing. While we were in Mexico we asked her if she wanted us to go back to the States if that would be the answer to make her feel better. She said no.

I do not believe that any sickness is from God. However, I do know that if we submit to God He takes very bad and seemingly unredeemable situations and works them for our eternal benefit. We have not accepted Aspen and David's conditions as inevitable and unchangeable. We will continue to believe and fight for their healing in prayer. We will never give up. If necessary, we will stand for their healing all the days of our lives, even if we never see a change.

> We will continue to believe and fight for their healing in prayer. We will never give up. If necessary, we will stand for their healing all the days of our lives, even if we never see a change.

Hebrews 11 lists men commended for their faith. Verse 13 says, "All these people were still living by faith when they died. They did not receive the things promised; they only saw them and welcomed them from a distance, admitting that they were foreigners and strangers on earth."

It's faith in God, not faith in an answer, that is most important. In Jesus' mighty name, we will stand unmoving in our trust in Jesus until we die. Jesus must be the focus of our faith.

We believe in miracles and we've seen great victories, and we thank the Lord for His strength to stand in the midst of trials. We have also suffered defeats. I like victories much more than defeats, but it is the defeats that give us the opportunity to not be moved no matter if we receive what we stand for or not. To *stand* unmoving is an effortless exercise if all we have are successes. Strength cannot be built without resistance.

All of our children seek God with their whole hearts despite the trials they have endured. Those things have tempered them and perfected them rather than hindered them. Each one of them chose to be made better from their suffering, not bitter.

Hannah is a healthy wife and mom embarking on life's adventures in God with her husband, Ben Johnson. They live in Colorado Springs and the two of them love the Lord and are teaching their two children, Hadassah and Samuel, to do the same. Hannah's like a walking concordance as the Word of God is deeply embedded in her heart and mind.

Aspen is running after Jesus with great vigor. If you meet her you will be inspired to know Jesus more. She graduated May 2015 from Auburn University along with her soon-to-be husband, John Marshall. She is working for Mountain Gateway as our Operations Administrator. In June 2016, while we were doing the final editing of this book, Aspen went to the ER in Wichita Falls, Texas, with acute abdominal pain and they discovered the source of Aspen's lifelong struggle. She had adult intestinal malrotation. They sent her by ambulance to Dallas where she had surgery to correct it. God orchestrated every step, and the best surgeon for this condition was her doctor. She is now walking in recovery and we pray and believe that she will know for the first time what it is to live pain-free.

Jacob did not die. The doctor told us that it was a miracle that he didn't since he'd been sick for so long with typhoid fever. Jesus is alive and so is our son! He has now grown strong and tall, and is married to his one true love, Cassie, and they are working full time with us. He loves God with all of his heart, and he and Cassie have surrendered their lives to the call of God.

David has had a great encounter with God and despite his physical pains he presses on with God's favor. He will be attending college soon. We are so proud of how he presses into the difficult and won't give up. He is a worshiping warrior who sees and hears what many do not.

I don't claim to understand the what or the why of all these struggles we have wrestled with for our children. I do know this: we must never give up. And we can never blame God.

We are commanded to give up our lives.[96] We are commanded to endure hardship. Paul says, "Join with me in suffering for the gospel, by the power of God."[97] Hardship produces suffering, and we are commanded to not grumble or complain as we walk and live out our lives in the strength of His joy.[98]

Having done all, *STAND.*[99]

---

[96] Matthew 16:24

[97] 2 Timothy 1:8

[98] Philippians 2:14

[99] Ephesians 6:13

22

Ordinary, Unschooled Men

I have walked countless miles in Mexico, alongside men the world is not worthy of. My mettle has been forged in the fires of mud and rain, walking beside these great men. I have seen the blessing of God carried by unknown champions. Their feet bear the Good News to the lost, and are beautiful, even though the bearing itself mars their appearance.

I know such feet, feet that have been broken, pushing these servants of Christ past their limit. Feet that have blistered and ruptured, bearing the weight of lost souls, driven by the blood of the Master to reach His goal. Feet that have cracked and bled, opening the next village for the Gospel. Feet whose toes are knots and whose nails are thick and marred from walking. Feet that have borne twisting and tearing, yet still care enough to walk so that the lost can be found and the dying can live, so the lame can walk, so the blind can see, and so those who are demon possessed and destroyed can be healed and set free.

This is the Gospel, the power of God unto salvation. Salvation is borne to the lost on feet that do not stop. We must walk and not faint, we must run and not be weary.[100] The lost must hear, and the dying must see that Jesus is alive, and He is God.

---

[100] Isaiah 40:31

227

Many times the advancement of the Gospel seems about as unspiritual an activity as you can imagine. It involves hours that turn into days and months, even years, of faithfully putting one foot in front of the other in spite of fear, disappointment, physical aches and pains, enemy opposition, and sweat. Lots of sweat.

In 2004 we were trying to establish a Gospel foothold in a village that required hiking to the bottom of a two thousand foot canyon—and of course hiking back up. Progress was slow, stretching out for months. I had to make the trip a dozen times before I found a person who would host us and listen regularly to the message of Jesus.

In September, during one of my visits to this village, I was told about a demon-possessed man who needed prayer in a village that was a four-hour hike away. A day and time were set for the visit.

In this area of Mexico there is a small radio station that broadcasts local indigenous programming. Part of the service this station offers is a verbal bulletin board where community announcements, requests, and messages can be broadcast. The man who had asked me to visit the possessed man used this radio station to announce that I was going to pray for the afflicted man and gave the day and the time I would arrive.

Since representatives of various religions, including witch doctors, pray for the sick and oppressed, this was not an unusual announcement. The radio announcer didn't mention that I was going to preach the Gospel though.

I arrived on the appointed day at the house of the demon-possessed man. As soon as this tormented man saw me, he screamed and ran off into the jungle, pulling his own hair in both hands. The demons that possessed his soul fled from the Holy Spirit I was accompanying to that place. This man's brother invited me to stay because he wanted healing for his brother, so I stayed for a couple of hours, sharing the Gospel with him and others in the family.

While we were sitting and talking, Francisco, a man from another village who had heard the announcement on the radio, showed up. He told us he had been trying to study the Bible by himself for years, and after I listened to him for a few minutes, it was obvious he was sincerely seeking the truth. Francisco knew the man who'd made the radio announcement and hoped that I had something different to offer than those who normally came to pray for the sick.

I shared the Gospel with this man and he accepted Christ! He then invited me to come to his village, and I scheduled a time to visit his house a few days later. I left that afternoon without having the opportunity to pray for the demon-possessed man because he had run off into the jungle and never come back. But, as always, God's plans are the plans that matter.

Francisco became a faithful disciple of Jesus. I hiked down yet another mountainside to go and see him and then continued to visit him and his family at his house every week. His wife and three daughters gave their lives to Christ too.

Each time that I arrived at their home Francisco was full of questions, and he became a sponge for truth. Years earlier he had taught himself how to read so he could study the Bible. He tried to get the local Catholic priest to teach him how to study the Bible but was told that he didn't have the capacity to understand on his own; it was the priest's job to teach the people what the Bible meant. Jesus answered his heart cry through a radio announcement and me showing up at his village with the Good News of the Gospel. God answers prayer!

I asked Francisco to prepare a message for a campaign, even though he had only been saved about three months. I gave him a month to prepare and helped him a bit with structuring his message. This nearly illiterate man worked and worked on his message.

The campaign day came and the house where we were having the service was packed with over eighty people. When it was Francisco's turn to preach he stood to his feet, literally shaking in his sandals. He held his written sermon in his hands and trembled so much that the paper shook like a leaf. He was so scared that tears streamed down his cheeks. He stumbled slowly through his message and sat down.

I was so proud of Francisco. He had overcome his fear and had the courage to speak of his faith to the crowd. Something happened inside of him that day. After that he began to share and preach more and more, visiting other villages with a burning desire to do the work of Jesus.

Francisco and I have walked numerous trails together and sat and reasoned with many people over the condition of their souls. As we hike together, I am constantly talking, and explaining, and teaching. As we have done countless visits together, Francisco has watched how the work of the Gospel is carried out and now he is leading people in four villages.

At times Francisco would accompany me three or four times per week, neglecting his fields because of his hunger to learn more about Jesus. He grew in his speaking ability and boldness and began to hold services on his own at his house, despite persecution from his community and his extended family. He led others to Jesus and began to pray for the sick and see them healed.

To this day Francisco is a piercing and bold light in a dark place.

Five years passed, and in late January of 2009, while Francisco was at his house preparing to hike one hour to meet me to go to a service in another village, he heard his grown daughter scream, "My baby is dead!" Her son, who'd been born six weeks earlier, was limp and lifeless. His daughter was terrified and weeping.

The first thing Francisco said was, "How can he be dead if Jesus is alive? Give him to me!" He took his grandson in his hands and walked outside his hut.

The grandson had no vital signs, no breathing, no pulse, no movement. Francisco describes him as being as limp as a dead chicken. He began to call out to God as he walked around and around just outside his house while his daughter sat devastated, crying inside the hut.

I had testified to Francisco about many people being raised from the dead in other places in Mexico where we worked with Freedom Ministries. He had come with me to visit the area where I used to work and had heard, firsthand, dozens of testimonies about the power of God. I had made sure that he knew what the Bible had to say about healing and the miraculous. We had seen astounding miracles in the area of Mexico where he lived as well, including people raised from the dead. He knew the story of Lupita, raised from the dead through the prayers of her father and mother.

I am blessed by the fact that our work for Jesus is built on an open show of the Spirit's power so that no man can lay claim to God's glory.[101] I had taught Francisco, now one of my main pastors, that the Gospel is both hearing and seeing, teaching and demonstration.[102] The Gospel is the power of God unto salvation.[103]

> If you take the power from the Gospel, all you have left is academic philosophical Christianity. We don't make converts to philosophy. We make disciples of Jesus, full of power that's demonstrated to souls who are lost and perishing.

---

[101] 1 Corinthians 2:4-5

[102] Matthew 11:4-6

[103] Romans 1:16

Words without power are merely philosophy without relationship. Relationshipless philosophy is only someone's argument. If you take the power from the Gospel, all you have left is academic philosophical Christianity. We don't make converts to philosophy. We make disciples of Jesus, full of power that's demonstrated to souls who are lost and perishing.

So as Francisco walked and prayed he held out his dead grandson, believing, pleading, asking, crying, doubting, and believing again. The prayer continued for about twenty to thirty minutes when, in the palm of Francisco's hand, he felt a tiny heartbeat! Life pierced death as that little one, locked in the final verdict of mankind, jerked when his heart started beating again. His arms and legs began moving, and he was given back his life from the dead!

Jesus is the resurrection and the LIFE!

Francisco only went through the second grade in school. He has no distinction that is evident by looking at him or hearing him speak or by seeing his home. He is extremely poor in terms of material possessions. He is, by anyone's account, ordinary and unschooled.[104] But Francisco is the living message of power to those who will listen. What makes him different is that this man has been with Jesus. It is Jesus who takes the ordinary and transforms it into the extraordinary.

I count it a privilege and an honor to know Francisco, who is so wealthy in faith and relationship with God.

As Scripture teaches, simple people are given the ability to understand profound, divine mysteries.[105] Humility attracts grace and opens

---

[104] Acts 4:13

[105] Luke 10:21

the door for the infinite complexities of God to transform a soul. Human knowledge inflates with arrogance and pride,[106] restricting the conduit to Heaven, blinding and deceiving the knowledgeable, in human terms, to the living truth.

I do not have the creative ability to explain how meaningful and spectacular it is to see these "simple" village people transformed into bold disciples of Jesus. All I can say is that Jesus is alive, and He has proven this in the work we are doing for Him.

The issue is transformation. Exactly what is this thing called life in Christ? Is it merely believing the right information as we construct ever expanding circles of moralistic expressions designed to give definition to our Christlikeness? Or is it to live and walk with a Lord who is risen and alive and real?

There is no revelation of Truth without Jesus living in us and transforming the way we think, believe, and live.[107] If there are deep theological ideas that are understandable by those who do not know Jesus, then it is not Truth they know and understand. What they understand are only philosophical and moral-code constructs given by God to humanity in order to give a platform from which to find Him. It is information only, and not the living Spirit of Truth that is promised to all who walk with God.[108]

Truth is not information! Truth is the Spirit of God.[109] That, and only that, is what sets us free.[110]

So many Christians seem to think that what gives spiritual life is the diligent study of Scripture or believing the right doctrine. Diligently

---

[106] 1 Corinthians 8:1-3

[107] Luke 24:45, John 14:26, John 16:12-14, Galatians 1:11-12

[108] 1 Corinthians 2:10-16

[109] John 14:15-17

[110] John 8:32

seeking Jesus with all our heart, mind, soul, and strength, which includes the study of Scripture, is what gives us life.[111]

I often thought while I was growing up that if I could have walked the earth with Jesus as one of His then-time disciples, I would have known the mystery of the Gospel, just like those whom Jesus used to reveal the Scriptures. As a young man I observed people moving from one church to another because they felt "like they were not being fed" or because another church could provide a better program for their kids. I began to realize that this motivation was human focused, not God focused.

If you know Jesus and you pray and worship, it does not matter where you are; you will be fed to ultimate satisfaction by His presence. But if our growth in God is dependent upon the gifting of a man and his ability to teach the Scripture, based upon his anointing or intellect or education or gifts or understanding of God, then no wonder our churches are weak and America is sliding into steady decay.

I'm not saying that you shouldn't want to go to a church that is preaching the Word and not merely telling stories, or that you shouldn't look for a church with a strong children's program. Those are great things. What I'm saying is that more than focusing on a man's style of preaching the Word, or what the church has to offer us, we must be a part of the body of believers where Jesus wants us to be.

The union of the Trinity of God the Father, God the Son, and God the Holy Spirit is beyond our grasp. The Father has sent Himself to interact with us by two agencies:

---

[111] John 5:39-40

First, He sent His Son to build the *impossible* bridge to Himself and to construct a doorway to the divine in a way that only God could have accomplished, a remarkable plan that empowers us to complete the journey to Him across the great sin divide.

Second, He dispatched His Spirit to make His habitation in us while we were still sinners in our imperfect state.

All of this spiritual activity is predicated upon one single fact, the acceptance of His Son. He decided to demonstrate His love to us by dwelling in us, knowing that we would continue to entangle ourselves in the webs of sin manufactured by our very own nature. He made the decision to give us an earthly path that would allow us to be perfected, to be sanctified in a lifelong process.

Only God Himself could provide for us to move through the entanglements caused by the corruption in the world because of evil desires.[112] He decided to put up with us and dwell in us because He knew there was no other way for us to reach Him in His glory. He knew that He would have to work from inside of us, to transform us from unacceptable to acceptable, to enable us to enter the ultimate expression of His love for us. So He fills us with His Holy Spirit.

We have erred greatly by demanding that theological study is the preferred means to understand sound doctrine. If you have studied theologically and are able to testify that your studies have been beneficial and find this statement offensive, please know that it is not my desire to offend. I will say, though, that if the Holy Spirit had not worked in your mind and heart in your studying, you would not have found one ounce of authentic understanding, regardless of all the time and money you invested.

If you have true understanding, it is because you have drawn close to Jesus.[113] However, the time and money that are required for studying

---

[112] Hebrews 12:1-3, 2 Peter 1:3-4

[113] John 5:39-40

in academia are not accessible to most of the world's population. God has provided the means for mankind to know Him purely from seeking Him in the simple structure of the local church.

The ministry that God has given us in Mexico has pastors who cannot read, or barely so, yet they live the reality of the Scripture. Some of them are subsistence farmers who live on only three dollars per day. Even if they could find some way to attend Bible school or seminary, the others in their family would starve. I am commissioned to teach them to obey the words of Jesus, not to send them away to a training institution to get prepared to advance the Kingdom. This is why I have a call to make them into disciples in the setting that works for them, and the results are extraordinary.

They win souls. They heal the sick. They make disciples. They raise the dead. They cast out demons. They cleanse lepers, and they do not charge for doing these things, exactly like the Bible commands.[114] What they teach through their preaching is sound and results in amazingly powerful acts by the hand of God.

Cristo vive! Jesus is alive!

---

[114] Matthew 11:1-6, Matthew 10:5-8

2 3

Kidnapped

In March of 2005, two months after the miracle of chicken and rice, Mario was at his cattle ranch, which was about a thirty-minute drive down the mountain from his house, working his cows on horseback. It had been his habit for years to go to his ranch three or four times per week to look after things.

On this day he was through with his work for the day and rode up to his horse trailer and dismounted. Mario was preparing to load up his horse and return to his house in town when six heavily armed men came out of hiding and surrounded him. Two of them had AK-47 assault rifles and the other four had .45 caliber semiautomatic pistols.

The kidnappers beat Mario, blindfolded him, and took off with him in his truck. They drove down a remote dirt road, deep into the jungle. Later they abandoned the truck, put a six-foot length of rope around the rancher's neck and dragged him like a pack mule off into the forest.

After stumbling along for a while, Mario convinced his abductors to take off the blindfold, which made it much easier for him to walk without falling. He walked behind some of his captors and the others were behind him. They were cruel and often shoved him in the back and then jerked the rope in order to keep him off balance. He held onto the rope around his neck to give some slack, because every time they jerked the rope he choked.

Although Mario had no idea if he would survive the kidnapping, a great peace seized his heart. He remembered how once we had begun a service by reading Psalm 91. So he prayed silently, "Lord, brother Juan (my first name is Jon and that is what they call me in Spanish) taught us not to pray to any other God but You. You said in Your Word, 'a thousand will fall at Your side, ten thousand at Your hand'. Lord, there are only six men here. Please show me the right moment to escape. Don't only show me the moment, but also give me the strength."

> A wave of power surged through his body that he knew was supernatural. His fear was swallowed up with courage.

Somehow, without his captors noticing, Mario slipped the rope off his head and kept his hand at his throat and continued to walk and act like the rope was choking him as they pushed and jerked him along.

They came upon a barbed wire fence in the forest and Mario knew this was the time to escape! A wave of power surged through his body that he knew was supernatural. His fear was swallowed up with courage. As four of the men crossed over the fence, he jerked the rope, which pulled the holder off balance. Mario then snatched the pistol from his closest captor as easily as disarming a baby. He shot into the air a few times and his captors panicked. One of them opened fire with his assault rifle, wildly empting a thirty-round clip at him from just about six feet away. No bullets hit Mario! Holding the pistol, he took off running. Something kept them from pursuing him, and he escaped even though he ran in plain sight of these terrorists for over a hundred yards on a twisted ankle.

The next day, when the authorities were led to the spot, they found a lot of blood and two thirty round clips taped together with their ends reversed so they could empty one clip, pop it out, flip it around and have a full clip of bullets ready. One of the clips was empty, with thirty empty brass casings littering the ground. The authorities determined by the large amount of blood in one spot that whoever shed that blood was in all likelihood dead. It seems as though instead of shooting Mario, the bullets were turned away from him and into the very men who intended him harm!

He will cover you with his feathers.
He will shelter you with his wings.
His faithful promises are your armor and protection.[115]

We were traveling and preaching in the United States when this incident happened. I felt prompted to call Mario one day, and it turned out to be the day after his escape.

When he answered the phone, he said to me, "Brother Jon, now I *know* that Jesus lives. I was kidnapped and Jesus gave me the power to escape. They had me in their power, and I escaped. In that moment, I was no longer thinking about money, or cars, or better business. I was thinking about my life and my family. I now know that material things are fleeting and life is precious."

In the aftermath of this intense experience with these wicked men, Mario's wife, Dani, was worried and did not want him to go back to his ranch. She feared that the same men would abduct her husband again. So she prayed that Jesus would care for the ranch and literally put their property in the hands of God. Her husband agreed and did not go near

---

[115] Psalm 91:4

his ranch for over a year. This was a significant decision since the ranch was one of their main streams of income.

As you can imagine, having a ranch requires a lot of work and attention. There were hundreds of cattle to be worked, and Mario usually spent three to four days a week, along with a ranch staff of six, tending to the cattle operation. Even with an education in veterinary and ranching science it took all of Mario's knowledge and effort to keep the ranch profitable.

One of the rancher's headaches for years was a flock of about two hundred buzzards that nested and lived on the ranch. Mario had spent fifteen years trying first one method and then another to get rid of them, with no success.

In his breeding herd there were many pregnant cows. As those cows would begin their labor to deliver a calf, the buzzards, ever vigilant and watchful, would communicate with the entire flock and prepare to descend en masse upon the unwary cow, just as the head of her newborn emerged. As labor progressed the buzzards timed their arrival perfectly so when the calf was delivered the birds viciously attacked the newborn. For obvious reasons the cow was unable to defend her young one, so the buzzards would peck out the eyeballs and tongue of the helpless calf, thereby setting up its certain death, and their next meal.

Mario and his cowboys had to be super attentive and on the spot at exactly the right moment in order to not lose calves in this way. This scenario had gone on for years, and the buzzard colony was effectively eating the profits.

This was just one of the many things that needed attention and coordination on his ranch. There were vaccinations, branding, fence work, peacekeeping with the neighboring ranchers, and the never-ending corral mending and expansion of outbuildings and feeding pens. All of this effort made Mario's presence a necessity. But because of his abduction, he did not set foot on his ranch for over a year. He assumed his losses during his absence would be disastrous, and he essentially gave up the operation in favor of preserving his life. He also let all but one of his cowboys go.

But God did not forget him. During all of those months not one cow or calf or bull died. And the buzzards left—never to return! The lone cowboy got lazy because there wasn't much for him to do. The fences stayed intact, the bulls behaved, and the cows gave birth in peace for *thirteen months!*

When Mario tells this story as part of his testimony, he says with a smile that Jesus is *el mejor vaquero,* the best cowboy!

This series of trying, yet redemptive, events changed Mario's perspective about life and galvanized his will to serve the Lord Jesus with his whole heart. He has remained faithful to this day. This man was not poor and needy like many others we have won to Christ. Still, as a "rich man," he has experienced many miracles. He is not one of the ordinary and unschooled men. But he has learned to lay down his life as well.

Jesus is no respecter of persons! His love and grace flow freely to anyone who will receive it.

2 4

The Work of the Holy Spirit

There never lived a more talented man than Jesus.

There never lived a man who could expound the Scriptures like Jesus.

There never lived a man who had a greater ability to communicate than Jesus.

There never lived a man who understood the mysteries of God better than Jesus.

There never lived a man who could flawlessly execute every nuance of the will of God more perfectly than Jesus.

There never lived a man as anointed as Jesus.

There never lived a man, nor will there be a man, who will ever match Jesus and His abilities.

So, if reaching the fulfillment of our place in God depends on the gifting, understanding, anointing, and communication abilities of our pastor or teacher, it would seem that Jesus' disciples would have grasped what He was teaching them during those three years they were together.

There never lived a better example for men to have than Jesus in the flesh. The disciples ate with Him and watched Him. They ministered beside Him and listened to Him teach every day. They walked beside Him while He had "skin" on. They had the ability to ask Him questions, and the benefit of knowing His personality. They saw how He did things. They understood the context of His human personality like we do not.

We tend to think that they had an advantage that we do not have. But Jesus told His disciples, and us, that it was better for us that He go away, so that the Father would send the Holy Spirit.[116]

We know that His disciples did not "get" what the most brilliant and capable teacher in all of history taught them. When Jesus died their world caved in upon them because they did not understand what He had plainly told them from the beginning of His time with them. Even after He rose again, they still did not understand, so He explained it all to them again on the road to Emmaus. And then again after He appeared to them while they were gathered. But they still did not get what He was saying, even though He was standing right there![117]

Then He did something miraculous, something mystical, something unprecedented. Luke 24:45 says, "Then he opened their minds so they could understand the Scriptures."

If we do not have this happen to us then no matter how talented our teachers are, or how great we make our learning institutions, the human mind and heart just do not have the capacity to understand the depth of the Scriptures.

After He gave them a supernatural touch and opened their minds so that they could understand the Scriptures, then and only then did they fully understand what He had taught and explained constantly, both

[116] John 16:7

[117] Luke 24:13-49

before He died and after. Now they had the capacity to understand. This happened by a transfer of power and not diligent study under a wonderfully informed teacher. Diligent study does not get us to the point where Jesus will decide to do this to us. Diligent seeking with our whole heart will.

Understanding the message of Jesus is impossible without the presence of the Holy Spirit in us. That happens only after you truly get born again. The Holy Spirit is the means that Jesus uses to open our minds so we can understand the Scripture. The presence of the Holy Spirit in us is the only means by which we can have the opportunity to live with God for eternity. The Holy Spirit gifts us with conviction.

Conviction works in us by giving us three things:

1) the ability and perspective to understand that we are sinners and what sin is

2) the ability to understand what Truth is and the perspective to stand and live in that truth and walk in righteousness

3) the undeniable assurance that judgment is coming[118]

Study alone can neither produce understanding nor activate transformation. The Holy Spirit is the exclusive revealer of the truth.[119] He teaches us the meaning of the written Scripture and reveals to us the heart of God. There is no other means to truly understand.

This is why our native pastors in Mexico can understand and experience the glories of God like they do. Jesus has touched them through the Holy Spirit and opened their minds and given them the ability to understand the Scriptures. That ability depends on them maintaining communion with Him. And so He grows them from glory to glory and

---

[118] John 16:5-16

[119] John 14:26, John 16:12-13

faith to faith. He does that for them without formal Bible or theological training. That is what I teach them. That is what they live out.

———

I don't mean to sound as if I don't believe that there is a function for people teaching the Word of God, there certainly is. But what I want to emphasize is that God wondrously allows each of us into an amalgam with His Spirit in order to work on this earth. Jesus has chosen and equipped us to do the works of the ministry. He is in us and gives us supernatural understanding of the truth and His message. We are ambassadors of the Kingdom of God, and we must carry the message.

We can have Jesus, by His Spirit, come to us and open our mind so that we can understand the Scriptures.

If you read Galatians 1:11-12 you will see that the Apostle Paul received his ability to understand the mystery of God from Jesus Himself. He did not go to an institute started by the eleven disciples. Paul did not get saved until after Jesus had ascended into Heaven, so he is perhaps our greatest example that we are not at a disadvantage in gaining spiritual maturity. The same Holy Spirit that chose Paul and filled him with revelation is the same One who will fill us with the *same* revelation. We can have Jesus, by His Spirit, come to us and open our mind so that we can understand the Scriptures. And we must *understand* in order to be fruitful and to fulfill what Jesus wants,[120] if we just will not get in His way.

---

[120] Matthew 13:19

If we will give up our lives and seek Him with all of our heart, we will find Him! To reduce this process to academic discussion leaves us with a hollow, substanceless shadow of something living, powerful, and unexplainable! The Bible says that the Word is *living*—a living miracle!

I certainly am not against education, but I certainly am for Jesus and His ability to do anything. I hope that I never stop defending the living Christ. I believe what I read in the Bible, just like it is written.

I have heard all manner of reasoning of why certain parts of the Bible do "not work" today. The origins of those sad doctrinal stands come from years of study in academic institutions. All I can say is that Jesus is alive! We must stop tampering with His inspired Scripture. No real understanding is possible without knowing Him. Without a personal relationship with Jesus, the content of His message is foolishness and unknowable, but with a relationship with Jesus, the content of His message is eternal life.

I am not the best or most talented person who could do the work Jesus has given me. Many people have much greater ability. However, the missionaries we have in Mexico are the only non-native people to do the work in the location where we have been sent. The people living there have no choice—*we're it* at this point.

I believe with the very code written on my genes that Jesus will do what He says. He will transform the people we minister to by His power in a supernatural way.

2 5

The Gospel Is the Power of God

In January 2010, I called a meeting of our main pastors to ask them to fast with me and seek God for His plan to know how to respond to the harvest we were experiencing.

At this meeting I went around the table and asked each one of these great men, "What do you want to do? God is moving among us. We are seeing new villages and new souls almost daily. Miracles abound. I need to know what you want to do."

They were listening intently.

I continued: "We have people saved in thirty-five villages. Do you want to draw back and maintain the places we have? We do not have enough workers to keep up with the needs we already have. I know that the work is costing you time and money and blood. I know that your resources are overstretched. But I also know that God wants to win this county, then the surrounding counties, and then the country."

The men shook their heads. They did not want to halt the momentum.

"Every step we take in God costs more. What do you want, to maintain what we have or keep following God as He drives forward? First, we must make the decision, without knowing the exact plan for how. First, you jump in with all you have, then God responds with His power. What will it be?"

As I listened to each man testify of the great things God was doing in his area, I thought how things had changed since I'd first come. Then I had known no one, and there were no followers of Jesus in all but two of the places where now there were fledgling churches. I listened to all seven of these faithful men as each stated with such conviction that they would follow God to wherever He took them.

I listened to the testimony of Cristobal whose little girl had been raised from the dead, as he talked about how, when we first began coming to his house, he had no words to say. That he literally could not think clearly and keep thoughts ordered in his head.

> If the Gospel we preach won't "work" for all people—the rich and poor, the young and old, the intelligent and ignorant, the literate and the illiterate, then I don't think we are preaching the Good News of the risen Lord.

He went on to explain how for years he'd worked in cities doing plumbing work with PVC pipe and had often glued pipe joints in confined places with little ventilation. Eventually he had to stop that work, because smelling the glue had affected his ability to think clearly.

He testified that as he began to study the Bible more, and specifically since the fire of God had broken out among us, that he felt consumed with the drive to leave his house and seek out souls for the Kingdom. Cristobal had begun to call out to God to heal his brain so that he could think clearly enough to preach and testify.

He reported that every time he preached he expounded longer and longer upon the truth and Jesus was healing his brain!

If the Gospel we preach won't "work" for all people—the rich and poor, the young and old, the intelligent and ignorant, the literate and the illiterate—then I don't think we are preaching the Good News of the risen Lord. If the doctrines taught from our pulpits require years of academic study to understand and then to teach, I think the message has been buried under the wisdom of man, wearing theological robes so thick that Jesus is barely recognizable, much less "experienceable."

I am so humbled and grateful to be a witness of Jesus and His wonders on this earth—*now*.

If we spent as much time, money, and effort seeking to know Jesus and obey His great commission as we do studying to ascertain which portions of Scripture do not apply today, we would have many more capable ministers leading the Kingdom charge into dark places.

As I have stumbled along, seeking God with all my being, I have encountered Him in an ever-increasing capacity. If we hold to the premise that He wants personal, vibrant, and miraculous relationship with us, then learning *about* Him leads *to* Him. That is as it should be. There is no end to Him! There is no end to the marvels that He will work, and that He will let us work with Him. If we ever find Him in any capacity whatsoever, it is only because He wants to be found.[121]

If we seek Jesus with all our being, we will find Him.[122]

All this is plainly written in Scripture. It is definitely okay to believe what you read in the Bible! The Bible works exactly as it is written if you let it lead you to Jesus.

———

It has been said that the man with experience is not at the mercy of the man with an argument. Based on so many miraculous healings, I

---

[121] Jeremiah 29:14

[122] Jeremiah 29:12-13

cannot be convinced that Jesus does not heal today or do other extraordinary things. I have been healed. I have seen so many others healed. I have seen Jesus do nearly all the sensational things talked about in the Bible.

I am well aware of the abuses and sensationalism of many people in this area. However, I also am well aware of what is written in the Book of books. If it is written in the Bible, no matter who tries to abuse it, then I will believe it.

Obey it. Die for it.

There is no one like Jesus. He can be trusted.

Hope in Jesus is never false.

The Holy Scriptures

Some people may read this book and conclude that I am anti-Bible. Nothing could be further from the truth. The testimony of God is in written form to lead us to encounter Him in real life by faith, not to be misapplied into academic pursuits.

I am not against learning or education. Indeed, we should submit ourselves to Jesus in all areas and learn throughout our life. There is an endemic drive in the soul that pushes us to connect with something greater than ourselves. The Truth that is Jesus beckons from every medium of communication that exists.

The written Word has been *the* constant authoritative guide for the growth of the Church worldwide throughout history. Jesus said to love Him with all our heart, soul, *mind*, and strength.[123] Any time we concentrate our seeking in only one area, at the exclusion of others, we slide into error and danger. We must seek God with all our mind, yet we must guard against the fact that the more we learn and know, the more danger we are in of exalting ourselves against God.[124] Knowledge can make us arrogant, and it was the desire for knowledge that led to the downfall of man in the Garden of Eden.

---

[123] Deuteronomy 4:29, 1 Chronicles 28:9, Matthew 22:37

[124] 1 Corinthians 8:1-3

> The Bible is not merely an ordered compilation of superior, enlightened ideas, or layers of philosophical webbing. It is the understandable message sent to show us the way to open the door to Jesus.

The Scripture does not give us eternal life, nor does the academic study of it bring enlightenment. The Scripture leads us to Jesus, and Jesus gives us Life. He *is* Life. His Life is our Light and brings enlightenment. His Word is living.[125]

The Word cannot be understood beyond its threshold, its invitation to know Him, without a relationship *with* Him. The Bible is not merely an ordered compilation of superior, enlightened ideas, or layers of philosophical webbing. It is the understandable message sent to show us the way to open the door to Jesus.

We base all of our life upon the Bible. Indeed, all of Western Civilization has its underpinnings anchored in the precepts of truth enunciated in the Word of God. The truth cannot pass away, because Jesus is the Truth, and His Spirit is the Spirit of Truth.[126]

The role of the written Word has been invaluable, even to those who cannot read, in so many lives among the indigenous people of Mexico. To have God's thoughts, opinions, and absolutes *written down* is astoundingly impressive once they grasp that reality. God is calling to us, and the fact that there is a book where that Truth is written down is *the* foundation for all else that emerges as these converts explore new life.

---

[125] John 5:39-40, John 14:6, John 1:4, John 8:12, Hebrews 4:2, 1 Peter 1:23
[126] John 14:6, John 14:15-17

I think God chose His Word to be written in order to give clarity in articulation—a source we can refer to time and again. It is the only resource that can be constant in content and intent regardless of the language or culture that the message happens to be wrapped in.

The Scripture is the testimony of Jesus. The path it leads us down inevitably brings about an encounter with Him, the living Word. The encounter works within us, to transform us from the inside out, compelling us to *become* something that we cannot be alone, but that we long to be with every molecule of our being. The Word changes us!

We have seen time and time again while working with our people in Mexico that the miracle of enlightenment dawns in their soul as they begin to read the Bible. This comes about not through mere education or via advancement to literacy, but through a transformation in thinking. Light begins to dawn in the obscurity of their mind and a fertility of ideas starts to explode and synthesize change in their thinking.

> **This comes about not through mere education or via advancement to literacy, but through a transformation in thinking.**

And it is change on every level. Critical thinking abilities emerge where none were evident before. Practical and innovative ideas start flowing, bettering their lives. They begin to have intuitive processing skills to reach solutions to problems that they and the generations before them never attempted to grapple with. The Bible is not just another book. It is the Book of books. Nothing else compares!

One story reveals how amazing this process often is. We met Juvencio, a young man who was a total drunk, who could not read, and whose life was a waste. Through a series of circumstances he turned his life over to Jesus. He had no schooling, except what his family had taught him in the normal course of life. Juvencio was completely illiterate.

After his conversion he had been accompanying me for several months as I went from village to village. One day, out of the blue, Juvencio asked me for a Bible. I was glad to give one to him, but was curious as to why he wanted one since he could not read, nor was there any obvious opportunity for him to learn.

He told me that somehow he was going to learn how to read. Some yearning inside was driving Juvencio out of his fear and intimidation and filling him with hope, determination, and courage. He was confident that he could learn! There was no teacher available, but somehow he stepped outside of his dead-end life with an intense desire to read about God for himself. Something calls us to draw close.[127]

About three months later I noticed that Juvencio was reading his Bible with apparent ease. Somehow, by himself, he had learned to read! I asked him a few questions and it became obvious that his teacher had been Jesus—because Jesus can do anything! This young man's whole countenance was utterly transformed. Where there had been nothing but emptiness in his face and eyes before Juvencio met Jesus, now his eyes shone with life. No amount of money could have purchased the smile that became the dominant feature of his countenance.

Jesus is alive!

—————

Some people may think that I am advocating miracles over attention to the Bible. I am not. I am advocating the idea that the study of the

---

[127] Ecclesiastes 3:11

Scriptures must lead to Jesus, the Jesus of the Bible, because the Bible is the testimony about Him. But I don't think there is much inherent value in the Scriptures apart from the risen Christ. Without relationship with Jesus, the Scripture will not give life. What is written in Scripture is the standard for living and the only unchanging, written truth about life in existence.

Miracles in and of themselves can never sanction a man's heart or ideas. Jesus worked many miracles in the midst of sinners. He still does that. Jesus had a betrayer on his team, and that same guy went out with the seventy disciples and worked miracles. Jesus will respond to people who seek Him, and He will use compromised vessels to work His will on this earth.

Too many spiritual leaders have been self-deceived by their own gifts and the effects of those gifts on others. Such leaders slide into thinking that they can compromise the standard of living that God demands in all its many nuances. For some, the compromise involves blatant disregard for standards of holiness and integrity. With others the misuse or misapplication occurs in the interpersonal life skills that Jesus taught so insightfully. In fact, we all have a corrupt nature, and our character is flawed and bent away from the original plan that God has for us. That is why we will always need Him.

We are given supernatural gifts, and they work because they drive to complete their intended purpose. They are energized with the power of God, the Giver of gifts. They will lead you if you let them. Their effect can fool you into thinking that your personal weaknesses are acceptable to God because the flow and power of your gift are so magnificent.

The Scripture must be the measure we use to gauge a man's status with God—nothing else can be the standard. Of all the writings in existence since time began, only the Holy Scriptures are inspired by God and are inerrant.

2 7

Visions

"In the last days," God says, "I will pour out my Spirit on all people. Your sons and daughters will prophesy, your young men will see visions, and your old men will dream dreams" (Acts 2:17).

On March 10, 1999, I had a service in the evening with another missionary, Shawn Williamson. We sensed that the Spirit of God was strong even before the service started as we shared a meal with the people.

After we got through eating at around 7:30 p.m., we walked down to the church building. The closer we got to the building, literally the more intense the presence of God became. His fire—His drive to save souls and work the miraculous—was a tangible, felt reality and affected all fifty of us gathered there that night. Every person who came to that service described it as "the fire of God." Shawn and the national pastors who were there went to the side of the building to talk about some situations that were occurring in some of the surrounding villages. I went and stood next to a small tree nearby.

All of a sudden I saw, with my physical eyes, the Lord Jesus standing in front of me.[128] The most sobering atmosphere materialized with

---

[128] Matthew 17:1-2

the Lord—severe in every respect. The Bible says that God is a consuming fire.[129] That is how it felt around Him on this day. He dominated everything in an all-consuming way. His majesty and intensity arrested all my attention. It was the most overwhelming experience I've ever had, and His presence permeated all things. He was looking at me with eyes of burning fire, just like the Bible says He has.[130]

The radiance of His presence consumed me. I felt as though Jesus was searching my every molecule, reading the genetic code of every gene in every cell of my body. If more people could just glimpse Him, so many issues that hold such importance in our lives would disappear in a fog of insignificance.

I wrapped my arms around the tree. I was transfixed. I was simply overwhelmed with the severity and intensity of the presence of the Lord. That was the last moment that I remember being cognizant of my immediate surroundings until I awoke four hours later at about 11:30 p.m., crumpled around the base of that tree. In the time I was "gone," this is what I saw and remember:

I saw the mountains, valleys, rivers, streams, and roads near where we were. Everything I could see was constructed of jewels: rough, raw, uncut, natural jewels. Everything before my eyes was made up of these jewels, all fitting together like a puzzle. Every mountain, tree, bush, stream, trail and road consisted of jewels, and each jewel had its own

> The radiance of His presence consumed me. I felt as though Jesus was searching my every molecule, reading the genetic code of every gene in every cell of my body.

[129] Hebrews 12:29

[130] Revelation 1:12-16

color, a fire that radiated light in a distinct color coming from inside. The jewel itself was the color of the light it radiated. Some of the colors I recognized, but many I did not. And all the colors combined to create a hue that I do not have the ability to describe.

I knew that the Lord was standing beside me, showing me all this.

As I gazed I saw the valley we drove through to get to the village that night. I was looking down from above at this valley when I saw someone I knew who used to be a missionary in Mexico. He had a rickety dry-rotted, two wheeled ox cart, which was being pulled by an old flea-bitten ox. The man had blinders over his eyes, but he thought that he could see perfectly. He was leading the ox, and the cart was filled to overflowing with jewels.

The man got to what seemed to be a line drawn in the ground, and as he crossed that line, all the jewels turned into water that drained out onto the ground and disappeared.

The man was very frustrated. He seemed exhausted from obtaining his small load of jewels, and then they just turned into water and vanished through the cracks in the boards of the ox cart. He threw up his hands and walked off and left the ox and cart, apparently never to return.

Then I saw that there were other former missionaries who were also trying to get carts or wagons full of jewels hauled out of valleys throughout the area. Everyone else also had blinders on, and in different ways they all lost their jewels too. Except for one man.

This man had a wagon, much like those seen in western movies. The wagon had four large, sturdy wheels and was pulled by four big mules. This wagon had a huge load of jewels. But the further out of the mountains that this man got with his wagon, the more jewels that he lost, until he only had one jewel left in his hand. All the other jewels disappeared, and even his freight wagon and mules were gone. He then left Mexico completely and made it to a place that I did not recognize.

The one jewel he still had with him burned brightly with colored fire. This man had a fevered, crazed look about him. He went into what looked to be a workshop and put the jewel on a special pedestal. Then he took up a steel mallet and some kind of specialized chisel. He began to cut this jewel, which was a little larger than a softball. Each time he made a cut, the fire of the jewel dimmed and another blinder scaled his eyes. He worked and worked with great skill as a gem cutter, but the more formed by his hand the jewel became, the more the fire went out, and the more blind he became.

He succeeded in cutting this jewel into a shape like a diamond or emerald that would be set into a ring. As the last cut was made, the last of the fire in the jewel went dead cold out. It kept its color for a few moments and then turned into a cheap, worthless piece of solid cement in the shape of a huge cut diamond solitaire that was big enough to fill the man's hand. He now had so many scales over his eyes that he could not tell he only held a cement replica of a real jewel. In his blind state he thought he was holding the most valuable stone on earth, but it was just a dull, cement imitation that only resembled the authentic by the shape it held. It was totally worthless, but he couldn't tell. He thought he held the most valuable jewel in the history of the world.

The man was so elated with what he had in his hand that he ran crazy showing first his friends, and then to anyone he met.

Understanding flooded my mind as I saw the final result of this man's arrogant tampering. Tampering had brought him blindness and that killed the life and value of something that was created with living light and fire. I knew this man in real life. He was a missionary who quit the mission field consumed with selfish ambition. He took the real jewels of God's gifts, the stones of altars that were to be built to God, and the calling of God for men, and took it upon himself to shape those stones![131]

---

[131] Exodus 20:25, Joshua 8:31

He used his experience, gained by many years of working on the mission field, and dared to mix his wisdom with the wisdom of God and shape the way the stones of God looked. He felt he would add value to the stone by giving it his definition of what it should look like. He saw little value in its raw, uncut shape. But by doing so, he totally ruined the stone, and brought blindness and deceit down upon his own head. He thought he held priceless wealth in his hand, but in reality he held something with no power or worth.[132]

I was smitten to the heart! *Lord, I would rather die than tamper with Your stuff!*

Then I found myself standing beside Jesus. We had grown to an enormous height. He took one giant step to the south, down to Guatemala. Somehow I was with Him as He stepped, although I was not aware that I had stepped. As the step was being made, I could see and hear where He was stepping. It was somewhere in the mountains of Guatemala. There was a giant hole in the ground in the shape of a funnel. It was black as pitch and no light or color except black was seen there. I realized it was a funnel straight into hell.

Millions of people were sliding down that funnel into hell. They were screaming and wailing, and tearing at the sides of the cavity, at themselves, and at each other, but they could not stop their slide into eternal darkness. Jesus stepped onto this hole, such that His foot completely covered it. I was on His left. He looked at me and asked, "Where are the ones I sent here to stop this?"

We took another step, south into the Andes Mountains. Again, there was a funnel into hell. Wailing and screaming people

"Where are the ones I sent?"

---

[132] 1 Corinthians 1:17

were slipping down and out of sight. Again, Jesus' foot covered the hole. He looked directly at me and asked, "Where are the ones I sent?"

We stepped again over to Africa where Jesus planted His foot on the mouth of a funnel to hell. "Where are the ones I sent?" He asked.

We stepped to spots all over the world, and each time over a funnel into hell, and Jesus just kept asking me, "Where are the ones I sent? Where are the ones I sent? Where are the ones I sent?"

I could not answer, for I did not know. I stood speechless with my head down.

Then He said to me, "Find replacements. Help them stay."

I do not know how I'm to accomplish this, but one day I will have an answer for Him.

———

Within the next six weeks I saw this vision replayed forty-two times. I had told David Hogan that I knew there had been more to the original vision, but I could not immediately recall what I was missing. But more details returned to my memory in the month following the initial vision.

I heard the terrifying sound of people screaming, moaning, and wailing as they were sliding into hell.

On March 13, 1999, I was driving into Mexico after briefly being in the U.S. when I heard the terrifying sound of people screaming, moaning, and wailing as they were sliding into hell. As I was driving, a scene unfolded in front of me. I could see to drive as well as see the vision at the same time, like the heads up display on a fighter jet.

This time I could see the ground itself was pulling in the people so they would then slide down these funnels into hell. The ground was moving like one of those moving walkways at an airport, pulling the people effortlessly down the funnel, and then dumping them off the bottom edge into hell.

They were being systematically drawn down with no one to stop the tide. Some people were lying on their backs. Some people were on their face. Some were aware, and some were unaware. Some people were trying to climb off the conveyer belt but they couldn't. Some were spinning and writhing in panic. Some sat in dazed despair.

There were also some who were marching toward the funnel systematically, their speed increased by the moving ground. These people were scattered throughout the larger sea of people being swallowed up. They had blinders on and were marching by cadence and had long round bars of cold gray steel in their hands. They had these bars turned horizontally and were using them to push people down the funnel. These soldiers were not screaming, but were most intent and organized as they pushed people into eternal punishment with them. I did not see these soldiers after they disappeared into the darkness, swallowed up by their own deception. They all marched blindly into the dark torment not made for men.

As I drove I wept uncontrollably and could hear again the Lord's words, "Where are the ones I sent?"

"Find replacements. Help them stay."

Jesus Is Calling

We must walk and not faint, we must run and not be weary. The lost must hear and the dying must see that Jesus is alive, and He is God.

In the year 2000, a head indigenous pastor and I were leading three new missionary workers through a mountainous region that enfolds thousands of hidden, unreached villages. The entrenched demon spirits that inhabit the people and places of that region want to destroy everyone who enters their area. Murder is in the hearts of the people we are trying to reach there and the resistance is constant.

We hiked three days through numerous villages. We preached a morning service, hiked to another village, preached a noon service, hiked to another village and then preached an evening service each day. We would spend the night at the pastor's house in the villages where we preached the evening services and rise early the next morning to continue hiking and preaching up through the mountains. On the fourth day, we departed early in the morning. For five hours we climbed still higher up into the mountains, then descended for two hours to a valley, and continued hiking for fifteen more miles in three hours—until we reached one of our churches. After ten hours we arrived with blistered and bleeding feet, worn out and not feeling very spiritual!

We ate with the pastor of the church, and then went to the small, one-room bamboo church building in his yard where the believers met.

We sat on a homemade wooden bench and waited on the members to arrive for church service. The only people who showed up were the pastor and his two daughters.

We had hiked for four days, the last day for ten hours, our feet were sore and blistered, and only three people came to hear the Word of God! I admit; I was not happy. My heart sank. I felt disappointed that we had gone through the effort we had, and none of the regular attendees came.

As soon as the service started I was overcome with the presence of Jesus. I crumpled to the floor feeling like I might melt into the ground. I looked to the back of this small remote church and saw Jesus standing there! Jesus was *there*—in a seemingly forgotten place of the world—watching as only eight of us, the three locals and the five of us who had hiked there, worshiped Him. He had come, just like He said He would, among two or three people gathered in His name.[133]

I lay there stunned to once again see my Lord. This was not a church known for dramatic happenings. It was a remote, small, and isolated place with only a few people saved. A place not forgotten by God.

Jesus has His attention on ALL the earth, and no one place carries more importance over the other. Oh, how we assess what to us is "strategic" when we weave together plans to try to follow what Jesus has told us to do.

Modern Missions has abandoned millions of souls, simply because we assess the "strategic" value of locations and judge them unworthy of our effort. The wisdom of man says to follow "the urban shift" so we can reach masses with less effort and less resources. Did Jesus say that? I went to a forgotten place—and ran dead into HIM.

---

[133] Matthew 18:20

Then I heard a sound. It was His voice, but not coming from where He stood but rumbling up the valleys and across the mountains through which we had hiked in the past four days. Although Jesus was standing nearby, His voice was coming from the dozens of villages that we had passed through or around during our long four days of hiking. His voice was calling from each of those villages. He was calling for workers to come and establish His name in those villages. There must be a witness, alive in a physical body, who names the name of Jesus in every place where people live together on the face of the earth.

Then the voice of Jesus spoke to me from all those villages at once and said:

> I am in every village, town, and city on this earth where My Name is
> not named as Lord, and I am calling.
> Calling specific people by name to come and breathe life to those who
> are dying.
> But so few hear Me call.
> Fewer yet respond.
> And still fewer remain, once they come.
> I am calling.
> Calling age after age.
> I have let you glimpse something real.
> Now go and sound My call.

On our trek of five days, we passed many villages where the people had never heard the Gospel. We passed in sight of a dozen or more on this day alone. We could not go to any of them because our days were full with the villages we were already working in. There was a limit to how many villages we could reach. That limitation was and is caused by one thing: the workers are few.[134]

Part of the reason I have written this book is that I hear the voice of Jesus calling—calling from thousands of villages, and towns, and cities at once, calling as I have never understood His call before. Calling names of individuals, from different walks of life, from different places and different ages. I hear the names as He calls them out in a voice that is as tireless as the stars and as patient as darkness, as consuming as all the suns in the universe and as undeniably compelling as a taproot that can break the densest granite. Jesus is calling out to His people to come to these villages, these unfamous places.

He is calling them by name. I hear them individually, all at once.

Come and establish My Name here, come and show the people My life.

Come and stand for the captives that die without hope.

I am calling you.

Come!

Long ago Jesus began calling as He ascended to Heaven, yet to this day so many tarry, refusing to lay down their lives. Their ears refuse to hear, stopped up by a Christian life that has become so comfortable, but deadening. Blindness afflicts them because *they* themselves are in their own eyes, and not Jesus. They are merely concerned with their own lives—selfishly alive, having laid down their Cross in the distant past. Some of them hear but still they wait while the lost remain lost and the grip of eternal hell tightens.

May the Master drive us out, for His command is to *go!*[135] He will use His oil to heal us from the great sitting disease that has crippled His

---

[134] Luke 10:2

[135] Matthew 28:16-20

Church. The answer is in the going. I urge you not to be clouds without rain[136] and trees without fruit,[137] only to have your efforts cast aside at the end and burned in the fires of the "should-have-beens."[138]

Your name is being called.

If we could see Him, we would die rather than deny His call.

So many throughout the world die without hope. Don't be the catalyst that grows their despair by your silence and absence. We must stop working against the harvest by our sitting.[139] The true Gospel advances in the skin of His new creations, borne out by the testimony of each life that the presence of Jesus has changed. That's you and me. Neither recordings, words on a page, nor images piped through the air or through a cable, can replace living testimony. The true Gospel cannot be reduced to bits or bytes that move along at the speed of light.

> The true Gospel advances in the skin of His new creations, borne out by the testimony of each life that the presence of Jesus has changed.

The Gospel is Jesus and His change in our lives lived out in front of those that He has called us to reach. Our favorite books can't sit and eat with the lost, can't lay hands on them and see them healed, can't cry with them and laugh with them. A webcast can't walk beside them and answer their questions as we hike to the next village to share the Good News. There is no substitute for our life lived in God's harvest field.

---

[136] Proverbs 25:14

[137] Jude 1:12

[138] John 15:5-6

[139] Matthew 12:30

No pretext about efficiency or multiplicity will spare the fire in the Master's eyes when you and I stand before him.[140] There is no understanding in Jesus for our part in allowing the lost of the world to remain lost. He demands that we execute the ministry that He has commended to us, to reconcile mankind to Himself.[141]

If you yet draw breath, *respond* to His call.

When the Son of Man returns, will He find us persistent in our sitting?

"Where are the ones I sent?"

He is speaking.
Can you hear Him? Are you listening?
The very molecules of the air are replete with His signature.
All creation moves and vibrates with His power.
Let Him catch you away.
He is calling.
Respond.
He is speaking.
Listen.
There is *no one* like Him.
YAHWEH.

---

[140] Matthew 25:31-46

[141] 2 Corinthians 5:18, Jeremiah 48:10

AUTHOR CONTACT

Get in touch with us. Apply to Mountain Gateway where we can help prepare you and then help you GO.

For more information go to: www.mountaingateway.org.

ABOUT THE AUTHOR

There are not enough pages in this book for me to honor a friend of one's lifetime...but I will give you what I can fit into this small space from the depths of my heart.

From childhood to manhood and on into eternity, this man will have run the race to win. Of all people that I have ever come to know, Britt is a man after souls for Jesus Christ. He is of the Truest Ambassadorship and his life, for as long as I can remember, has been about following JESUS CHRIST! I know of no one else, shy of his own family, who are missionaries, that are really willing to let go of this life and die to self every day for the sake of others.

I have known him since he was a young boy, but he was never like any other child. The best biblical reference to his childhood I can give witness to is John the Baptist. It was as if Britt received the Holy Spirit in the womb. I don't know when that really happened, but Britt was raised in a unique place and, from what I remember, he was always full of God. I feel part of this is a tribute to Britt's parents and siblings. Their home outside of Birmingham was host to thousands of youth during the time referenced in the movie *Woodlawn*. The Hancocks have always walked with God and have been among the most generous and loving people I have known. Every one of them has lived for Jesus!

Britt became a woodsman as a young child and taught himself much about the outdoors. He was becoming a mountain man, even in the lower foothills of Alabama. Britt's lifetime journey with God has led him into many mountainous regions, and along the way he and members of his family have trained with NOLS, the premier school for backcountry skills and leadership training. Britt successfully completed the NOLS professional outdoor education training through their Mountain Instructor Certification Course.

In 1989, Britt founded Servant Ministries; in 2009, he and his wife, Audrey, founded Mountain Gateway where the decades of mission field experiences, training and intimate time and walk with God are used to raise young missions-hearted youth for a lifetime after souls and presenting the Gospel of Jesus Christ to remote regions. God has continually prepared Britt for what is in front of him and God has always upheld what He is doing with Britt, which is another personal testimony. He has spent hours alone with God worshiping, praying, walking and talking.

Today he has traveled much of the world and lived in some very diverse and remote places. Jesus was forging this man from his youth and while Britt has experienced more than most will encounter in a life-time...his is not over, but only beginning.

Britt would never write a book unless God was inspiring it by His Spirit. Given that, anyone reading this book is beneficiary to testimony and to teaching that one can only obtain from a loving, obedient walk with God by the Holy Spirit over years. The depths and the wealth of our King are revealed over time to the children of the Most High God.

I submit this on behalf of my dear friend Britt with petition and prayer that each reader will receive the personal Intention of God for their life from the Holy Spirit in Jesus' name!

Bruce R Wagner Sr. / CEO
Rapid Deployment LLC

NOTES

NOTES